A FIELD **GUIDE**
COMMON **BIRDS**
OF THE **INDIAN** SUBCONTINENT

A FIELD **GUIDE**

COMMON **BIRDS**

OF THE **INDIAN** SUBCONTINENT

ANANDA BANERJEE

RUPA

Published by
Rupa Publications India Pvt. Ltd. 2008
7/16, Ansari Road, Daryaganj
New Delhi 110002

Sales centres:
Allahabad Bengaluru Chennai
Hyderabad Jaipur Kathmandu
Kolkata Mumbai

ISBN: 978-81-291133-8-2

10 9 8 7 6 5 4 3

Cover and book designed and typeset by Arrt Creations, New Delhi

Printed at Gopsons Papers Ltd. Noida

Anand Arya

CONTENTS

N.C. Dhingra

ACKNOWLEDGEMENTS

I would like to thank the following for their support and help.

Kapish Mehra of Rupa & Co who came up with the idea of this book.

The photographs of the two hundred species that make up this guide book are the lifetime work of most beloved friends: N.C. Dhingra, Nikhil Devasar, Clement M. Francis, Dr Dipankar Ghosh, Satpal Gandhi, Anand Arya, Debashis Deb, Joydip & Suchandra Kundu.

Moreover, my interest in birds and natural history would not have intensified without the love and support of the following people: G.V. Reddy, Bikram Grewal, Mike and Ranjana Pandey, George Archibald, Bill Harvey, Sumit Sen, Sujan Chatterjee, Gopinath S., Dr Amitabh Diwvedi, Dr Rajesh Gopal, Shyamal Tikkadar, Avneesh Makkar, Manoj Kulshetra, Abhishek Ray, Kushal Mukherjee, Kanwar B. Singh, Himanshu Malhotra, Amit & Neha Verma, Haripal Singh Gill, Aditya and Poonam Singh, Vikram Singh, Mohan Singh, Dharam Singh, Fateh and Adil Singh Akoi, Prithvi and Umed Singh Gill, Pradip Vyas, Anil and Puja Ahuja, Subhabrata Bhattacharyya, Mike and Annie Vickers, Karan Bisht, Shiv Singh Mann, Tariq Aziz, Ondra Abonyi, Ansar Khan, Sumanta Ghosh Dilshad (Chottu), and especially, Indrani Rajkhowa Banerjee.

N.C. Dhingra

FOREWORD

Humans share this earth with a great variety of fascinating birds. Observing birds and identifying the species is a growing pastime in many nations. After gardening, bird watching is the most popular recreational activity in my country.

In India, 1,250 species of birds have been reported. Species that are uncommon or with limited distributions are seldom seen by the average person. However, other species are abundant with broad distribution and are readily observed. It seems that wherever you are in India, both in urban and especially in rural areas, there are birds.

Identifying a bird species is like remembering the name of an acquaintance. Such knowledge is pleasurable. As one practises the identification of birds, they soon become like good friends and bring great joy.

This attractive field guide by Ananda Banerjee identifies over two hundred of the most common species.

Dr George Archibald
(Co-founder, the International Crane Foundation)

INTRODUCTION

THE PLEASURES OF BIRD WATCHING

For centuries, birds have held a fascination for the human world and have been a subject of study. Ancient civilisations worshipped birds as gods and attributed magical powers to them in stories, fables and mythologies. Even today, these winged wonders inspire great awe, especially for their ability to fly, their ability to build extraordinarily intricate nests, and not least, the brilliant colours of their plumage—features that no human being can replicate.

Scientifically or taxonomically birds are categorised in 'orders', 'families' and 'genera' but overall they are divided into two groups: *passeriformes* (or passerines) and non-*passeriformes* (or non-passerines). Roughly sixty percent of all bird species are passerines or songbirds. Their most distinguishing characteristics are the specialised leg structure, vocal structure, and brain wiring, which allow them to produce complex songs. The non-passerines comprise twenty-eight out of the twenty-nine orders of birds in the world.

Other than leaving us wonderstruck, birds constantly remind us about our environment and how we have affected it and watching birds is a natural way to study and understand nature and our habitat.

Bird watchers come from all walks of life. There are as many varieties of bird watchers as there are birds. They range from professionals who travel across the oceans just to see a rare species, to the casual weekend hobbyists who enjoy watching the neighbourhood birds. The pleasures of bird watching stem not only from admiring the myriad shapes, forms, colours, behaviours, and songs of birds, but from the satisfaction in recognising their different species.

Bird watching always presents an intellectual challenge because there are so many different species to identify! Moreover, some birds due to their furtive nature pose great difficulties for the bird watcher. Very often one needs to put together bits and pieces of incomplete clues to come up with the proper identification. And mind, one doesn't always have the fortune of a good, long look at the restless creature. Problems of bird watching abound—sometimes most of the torso is hidden behind foliage or the moment you spot it the tiny creature is all set for flight or the sun simply refuses to shine brightly enough! So, to be a birder you need loads of patience and a deep love and respect for the winged species.

Early morning is typically the best time of the day for birding since many birds are active and searching for food, thus making it easier to spot and observe them. Identifying a 'life bird' (one you spot for the first time) by yourself can also give you a big boost. Adding species to your life list can become a great game to play. It can be competitive among friends and birding companions, or you can compete just with yourself. Not to mention the hand-to-eye coordination that you will have to develop while training binoculars on a moving object. Your movements have to be fast enough to focus your binoculars within milliseconds of spotting a bird. Expert birders are not born; they hone their skills progressively with time and practice.

Bird watching requires pin-drop silence and inconspicuous presence. Equipped with binoculars a birder should walk as stealthily as a cat. One can make use of the foliage, trees and bushes. It is often a good idea to take up position on the edge of a forest clearing or near fruiting trees. Lakes and large water bodies are excellent places for the wintering waterfowl.

Bird watching is a self-rewarding experience in India. There are many species to be seen and many different habitats to be visited all around the year. Bird watchers also take part in censuses of bird populations and their migratory patterns by counting all the birds in a given area. Amateur or avocational birders have contributed and continue to contribute much to the scientific knowledge of birds. They can also assist professionals in identifying environmental threats to bird life. Birds are by far the best touchstone for assessing ecological imbalances. Bird surveys help ornithologists and conservationists understand more about birds as well as the environment that we all share and depend upon.

BINOCULARS

The most important accessory or the utmost necessity for bird watching is a good pair of binoculars. Binoculars come in different shapes, sizes and weights. They are described by the magnification power and the size of the objective lens (for example: 10x42, 7x37, 8x40, 10x50). The first number indicates the number of times the image is magnified, and the second number is the diameter of the objective lens in millimetres.

I would personally recommend a specification of 8x40 of any good brand. These will help bring the bird closer to you optically so you can discern a bird's field marks, plumage pattern and colour better, as well as the subtleties of its behaviour. While good optics may be expensive, the choice of brand is very individual. A good guideline is to buy the best optics you can afford. Remember, before purchasing, it's important to try them out yourself. When testing, use each pair to focus on the same object, paying special attention to the detail of the image in the centre and on the edges.

Avoid binoculars that zoom, or that focus each eyepiece separately. For birding, these types of binoculars are only hindrances. It will be good to keep in mind that binoculars are a long-term investment, so you must enjoy using them. They should enhance your experience and never be a burden for you.

Watching wild birds is fun. Some birders even travel the world to add another 'lifer' to their list. Birding is more than a pastime—it is an adventure. The adventure can even start in your garden or in your backyard. Out of over 9,600 species of birds in the world the Indian subcontinent alone is home to over 1,200. Here, we describe more than two hundred of the most common birds that you will be able to start with in the spectacular avian world.

POINTS TO REMEMBER WHEN BIRD WATCHING:

- ☑ Take care not to disturb either the birds or their habitat. Walk softly on the land.
- ☑ Stay on established pathways and keep motor vehicles restricted to the roads and parking areas.
- ☑ Avoid harassment; do not disturb birds that are nesting or their nesting areas.
- ☑ Do not handle eggs or the young or stay too long at a nest side.
- ☑ Avoid tree-banging to arouse cavity dwellers. Undue disturbance may cause the bird to abandon its nest and young or even kill the young inadvertently in an attempt to escape.
- ☑ Divide larger groups of people into smaller, more manageable numbers. Small groups cause less disturbance and noise.
- ☑ Leave no litter or trash. Pack your garbage out of wilderness areas. Ingested items can kill.
- ☑ Support local and national bird conservation organisations.

BIRD **ANATOMY**

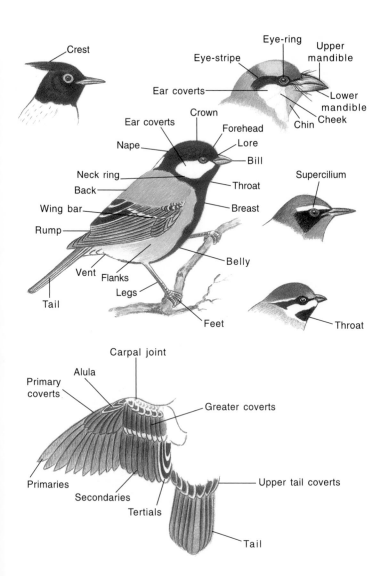

Crest

Eye-ring
Upper mandible
Eye-stripe
Ear coverts
Lower mandible
Cheek
Chin

Ear coverts
Crown
Nape
Forehead
Lore
Bill
Neck ring
Throat
Back
Wing bar
Breast
Rump
Belly
Vent
Flanks
Legs
Tail
Feet

Supercilium

Throat

Carpal joint
Alula
Primary coverts
Greater coverts
Primaries
Upper tail coverts
Secondaries
Tertials
Tail

DIFFERENT TYPES OF **BILLS**

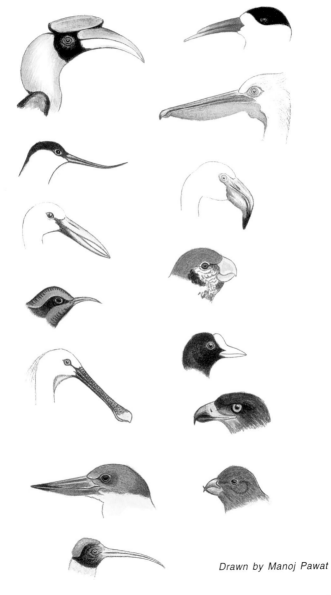

Drawn by Manoj Pawat

Satpal Gandhi

GALLIFORMES

Satpal Gandhi

CHUKAR (AROUND 38 CM)
SCIENTIFIC NAME: *ALECTORIS CHUKAR*

This beautiful stocky bird has a striking black eye-stripe extending across and encircling the neck. Chukar has a distinct red bill and legs with black and brown rib-like stripes on its sides. It is found in the mountainous regions of Pakistan, the Himalayas, and on rocky surfaces. It is also known as Chukar Partridge, and is the national bird of Pakistan.

BEST SIGHTED AT: Rocky landscape along mountain paths and near water bodies.

BLACK FRANCOLIN (AROUND 34 CM)
SCIENTIFIC NAME: *FRANCOLINUS FRANCOLINUS*

Also known as Black Partridge, the male is a plump black game bird sporting a white patch on the ear and white spots all over the body. A broad yellowish brown collar separates the head from the

body. The female is much paler with a brown patch on the back and a white patch below the eye. It lets out a loud, high-pitched *chee-chee keray bee* (sounds as if it's crying 'paan-beedi-cigarette'), a cry that reverberates across the landscape.

BEST SIGHTED AT: Cultivated fields and tall grasslands.

Debashis Deb

GREY FRANCOLIN (AROUND 33 CM)
SCIENTIFIC NAME: *FRANCOLINUS PONDICERIANUS*

Joydip & Suchandra Kundu

Also known as Grey Partridge, it is similar to Black Francolin in structure. It is grey-brown all over with buff on the throat underlined with black and a chestnut coloured tail. Grey Francolin is found across the subcontinent. Its high-pitched *khateeta khateeta khateeta* gives away its location easily.

BEST SIGHTED AT: Dry grasslands and scrub bushes.

RED JUNGLEFOWL (AROUND 70 CM)
SCIENTIFIC NAME: *GALLUS GALLUS*

Joydip & Suchandra Kundu

This is the fabled rooster with the well-known *cock-a-doodle-doo* and the father of today's poultry with its trademark red comb and wattle. One can only marvel at its beautiful, iridescent and multicoloured plumage. It has a red eye patch, golden yellow mane, and long, curved, green-black tail feathers. The female is much smaller in size than the male and is rufous brown in colour. It lacks both the comb and wattle.

BEST SIGHTED AT: Usually in groups of one cock and several hens around forest edges and undergrowth. Distributed all across the Gangetic plain but not present in south India.

BIRD TRIVIA
RAREST BIRDS IN THE WORLD: Ivory-billed Woodpecker (supposedly extinct) and Jerdon's Courser.

Clement M. Francis

GREY JUNGLEFOWL (AROUND 75 CM)
SCIENTIFIC NAME: *GALLUS SONNERATII*

The bright and striking male is heavily streaked in white and yellow spots while the much-smaller female is streaked only in white. Its deep red comb is slightly dented and its long neck hackles range from dark grey to a deep black, with yellow and white stripes running the length of the neck. The tail and back feathers are similarly coloured. Found only in peninsular India and indigenous to southern and western India, Grey Junglefowl is a close cousin of Red Junglefowl.

BEST SIGHTED AT: Bamboo forests and forest undergrowth.

INDIAN PEAFOWL (AROUND 200 CM)
SCIENTIFIC NAME: *PAVO CRISTATUS*

The national bird of India, it is a beauty to be watched at leisure. The shimmering and flickering blue-green plumage of the male comprises the longest spectacular tail, which has copper, green and blue discs. The half-sized brownish female lacks all of these and has a white face and throat. It has a little of the male's metallic green sheen at the back of its long neck.

BEST SIGHTED AT: Cultivated villages, undergrowth and deciduous forests.

N.C. Dhingra

4

ANSERIFORMES

GREYLAG GOOSE (AROUND 80 CM)
SCIENTIFIC NAME: *ANSER ANSER*

Debashis Deb

A large grey-brown goose, it has a large head and pink bill that is almost triangular. It is easily identified in flight by the pale grey forewings, pink legs and white rump. An ancestor of the domestic goose, Greylag Goose is a winter visitor to the Indian subcontinent and moves in large noisy flocks from late November to March.

BEST SIGHTED AT: Wetlands, large lakes and water bodies.

BAR-HEADED GOOSE (AROUND 75 CM)
SCIENTIFIC NAME: *ANSER INDICUS*

Nikhil Devasar

Another large wintering goose, it has a distinct double black band on the head and a white line on its grey neck. Its bright yellow bill has a black tip. Its blackish flight feathers with the grey body are distinctive in flight. It grazes on grass and can be spotted from late November till March. It breeds in Ladakh.

BEST SIGHTED AT: Wetlands, large lakes and water bodies.

BIRD TRIVIA | **FASTEST-MOVING BIRD:**
The diving Peregrine Falcon at 188 km/h.

Satpal Gandhi

RUDDY SHELDUCK

(AROUND 62 CM)
SCIENTIFIC NAME:
TADORNA FERRUGINEA

Also known as Brahminy Duck, it is seen in large numbers during winter months. It is warm buff-brown in colour with a cream coloured head. The fore wings are white and the wings have a dash of green. The male has a distinct black band across its neck. It is the only duck that spends more time on land than in water.

BEST SIGHTED AT: Wetlands, rivers and lakes.

COMB DUCK (AROUND 65 CM)
SCIENTIFIC NAME: *SARKIDIORNIS MELANOTOS*

The male Comb Duck sprouts a comb during breeding period and is much bigger than the female. It has a white head specked with black and white under parts. There is a black stripe from the crown to the mantle and also on the shoulder. The male's wings are iridescent blue-black and green, while the female has dull under parts and only green on its wings. It is a local migratory bird along the subcontinent.

BEST SIGHTED AT: Usually four or five female ducks are seen with a single male around wetlands and lakes.

Nikhil Devasar

GADWALL (AROUND 41 CM)
SCIENTIFIC NAME: *ANAS STREPERA*

Another wintering duck, Gadwall is found across the subcontinent. The breeding male is a beautifully patterned grey with a black rear end and a brilliant white speculum. The smaller female is light brown with black scaly marks and a dark orange-edged bill; it also lacks the white speculum.

BEST SIGHTED AT: Wetlands and lakes.

Anand Arya

EURASIAN WIGEON (AROUND 48 CM)
SCIENTIFIC NAME: *ANAS PENELOPE*

Clement M. Francis

The male Eurasian Wigeon stands out amongst the duck flock with its bright chestnut brown head and yellow forehead and crown (which looks like a *tilak*). It is a vermiculated grey all over with a pinkish breast and a black rear. The female is a relatively uniform brown with chestnut sides and a white belly. One of the noisiest ducks (the male has a sharp whistle), it is sighted during winter migration.

BEST SIGHTED AT: Wetlands and lakes.

BIRD TRIVIA
FASTEST-FLAPPING FLIGHT:
White-throated Needletail (swift) at 170 km/h.

SPOT-BILLED DUCK (AROUND 60 CM)
SCIENTIFIC NAME: *ANAS POECILORHYNCHA*

Clement M. Francis

This dabbling duck has a distinct yellow tip on a grey bill with red spots at the base. It is scaly grey to dark brown and its dark crown and eye-stripe make it easy to spot. One of the commonest ducks to be found, it is widely distributed all over the subcontinent.

BEST SIGHTED AT: Wetlands and lakes.

COMMON TEAL (AROUND 36 CM)
SCIENTIFIC NAME: *ANAS CRECCA*

Eddie Myers

This beautiful small duck has a chestnut head with a broad dark green band bordered by white lines around its eyes. Overall it is grey-barred and a broad yellowish patch is distinct on the under-tail. The female is more uniform in various hues of grey-brown and a black eye-stripe. It stays in large flocks.

BEST SIGHTED AT: Wetlands and lakes.

GARGANEY (AROUND 39 CM)
SCIENTIFIC NAME:
ANAS QUERQUEDULA

This is a widespread winter visitor to the subcontinent. A striking white stripe behind the eye makes the male Garganey stand out in a crowd of ducks. It is finely patterned brown on the throat and grey-white on the flanks and belly. The female Garganey resembles the female Common Teal except for its distinct white throat and lack of speculum.

BEST SIGHTED AT: Wetlands and lakes.

Anand Arya

NORTHERN PINTAIL (AROUND 54 CM)
SCIENTIFIC NAME: *ANAS ACUTA*

With its dark chocolate brown head and a long grey and black bill, this bird gets its name from the long, pin-like central tail feathers (a very distinct field identification mark). A vertical white band runs on both sides of its head merging into the white of the long neck. A brownish tone and lack of grey stripe on the bill clearly distinguish the female from the male.

BEST SIGHTED AT: Wetlands, marshes, and lakes.

Ananda Banerjee

BIRD TRIVIA **HEAVIEST AND TALLEST BIRD:** Ostrich at maximum 156 kg and 2.7 m.

NORTHERN SHOVELLER (AROUND 48 CM)
SCIENTIFIC NAME: *ANAS CLYPEATA*

(Male) (Female)

Ananda Banerjee

It is easily distinguished by its unique large shovel-like bill, which it uses to strain water from small aquatic plants and animals. The male has a dark green head (which almost looks black in poor light), rusty brown sides and belly and a white breast. The female is streaked in black and brown all over. This bird is the first amongst winter visitors arriving in large numbers and is also the last to leave.

BEST SIGHTED AT: Wetlands and lakes.

COMMON POCHARD (AROUND 47 CM)
SCIENTIFIC NAME: *AYTHYA FERINA*

This duck has a dome-shaped, chestnut brown head and it is finely barred with grey all over. The black breast and grey patch on the bill

add to its singular look. The duller female has brownish head and breast with brown-grey body. A winter visitor, Common Pochard is not found in Sri Lanka.

BEST SIGHTED AT: Wetlands and lakes.

Anand Arya

10

Anand Arya

TUFTED DUCK

(AROUND 43 CM)
SCIENTIFIC NAME: *AYTHYA FULIGULA*

The male Tufted has a glossy black head and body with white flanks and belly. It sports a hanging black crest on the head. The female is dusky brown in colour. Both sexes have yellow eyes and grey bill. Sometimes the female has a circular white face patch.

BEST SIGHTED AT: Wetlands and lakes.

LESSER WHISTLING DUCK (AROUND 42 CM)
SCIENTIFIC NAME: *DENDROCYGNA JAVANICA*

A small duck, it utters a shrill whistling note in flight. It is buff in colour with a distinct dark brown patch on the crown. It has a buff-scaled black back and rufous belly. The fore wings and upper tail have a chestnut patch. It is also classified as part of 'Treeducks' and is put into a different family: *Dendrocygnidae*.

BEST SIGHTED AT: Freshwater and wetlands.

Nikhil Devasar

BIRD TRIVIA

HEAVIEST FLYING BIRD:
Great Bustard at maximum 21 kg.

11

PICIFORMES

GREY-HEADED WOODPECKER (AROUND 32 CM)
SCIENTIFIC NAME: *PICUS CANUS*

Joydip & Suchandra Kundu

This woodpecker is overall pale greenish olive with a grey head and face. The male has a red patch on the black crown that extends to the nape. The female's crown is just black. It has a high-pitched *peeek peeek peeek peeek* that fades gradually. Woodpeckers hold on to the tree trunk with their forked toes and bore rapidly into it causing a drumming sound.

BEST SIGHTED AT: Forests in the Himalayan foothills.

Joydip & Suchandra Kundu

GREATER FLAMEBACK
(AROUND 33 CM)
SCIENTIFIC NAME:
CHRYSOCOLAPTES LUCIDUS

A big golden woodpecker with a red crest (in male) and black and white spots around the hind heck, it has a scarlet rump and a black tail. The female has a black crest. Its larger size, four toes (instead of three) and two distinctive black malar stripes (instead of one) differentiate it from its similar looking cousins, Himalayan Flameback and Common Flameback.

BEST SIGHTED AT: Broadleaved forests and mangrove forests.

BLACK-RUMPED FLAMEBACK (AROUND 27 CM)
SCIENTIFIC NAME: *DINOPIUM BENGHALENSE*

Nikhil Devasar

Found across the subcontinent, it is similar to Greater Flameback but smaller and has a black rump instead of scarlet. The black stripe around the eye is much thinner and it lacks the malar stripe. It even lacks the white spots around the neck and its throat is streaked with black. Its wings tend towards olive and the black wings have white patches.

BEST SIGHTED AT: Forests, wooded areas, and cultivation.

RUFOUS WOODPECKER

Debashis Deb

(AROUND 25 CM)
SCIENTIFIC NAME: *CELEUS BRACHYURUS*

This is a brown medium-sized woodpecker with a black bill and it is barred with black on the mantle, wings, lower flanks, and tail. The male has a red ear patch. It has a shrill *keenk keenk* sound and its drumming sounds are distinctive.

BEST SIGHTED AT:
Forests, especially near ant and termite colonies.

BIRD TRIVIA **LONGEST WINGSPAN:** Albatross at up to 3.63 m.

13

COPPERSMITH BARBET (AROUND 17 CM)
SCIENTIFIC NAME: *MEGALAIMA HAEMACEPHALA*

Clement M. Francis

A cute little dark green bird with a brilliant red forehead and breast patch, and bright yellow throat and eye-ring. Its call *tuk-a-tuk-a-tuk* can be heard from afar and it has to be spotted by following the call. As they sit amidst the thick canopy of leaves, this is the best way to track all barbets.

BEST SIGHTED AT: Gardens, neighbourhood trees, wooded areas.

BROWN-HEADED BARBET (AROUND 27 CM)
SCIENTIFIC NAME: *MEGALAIMA ZEYLANICA*

Anand Arya

A large green barbet with distinct brown head, upper back and throat, which are streaked with white. It has a big red-orange bill and a yellow-orange patch around the eye. The legs are orange too! It has a high-pitched call that goes *kutroo kutroo, kutroo kutroo.*

BEST SIGHTED AT: Trees near human habitation or cultivation, and in wooded areas.

BLUE-THROATED BARBET (AROUND 23 CM)
SCIENTIFIC NAME: *MEGALAIMA ASIATICA*

The face and throat of this barbet are aqua blue with a distinct red crown extending up to the nape with one black and one yellow patch across the crown. Overall green, it has a tiny red scrap near the chest. Its call is a loud and continuous *took-a-took*.

BEST SIGHTED AT: Himalyan foothills in northeast and eastern India, and well wooded areas.

Debashis Deb

INDIAN GREY HORNBILL
(AROUND 50 CM)
SCIENTIFIC NAME: *OCYCEROS BIROSTRIS*

A widespread resident across the subcontinent except in Sri Lanka, it is a grey bird with an oblong head, which is bigger in proportion to its torso. It has a huge black curved bill with yellow streaks. The diagnostic feature is the small black casque (also called 'horn') on the top of the bill. The wings and long tail have white terminal edges preceded by black. It hops around on tree branches in its characteristic clumsy manner.

BEST SIGHTED AT: Fruiting trees.

Anand Arya

BIRD TRIVIA

MOST TALKATIVE BIRD:
African Grey Parrot with a vocabulary of a thousand words.

15

MALABAR GREY HORNBILL (AROUND 45 CM)
SCIENTIFIC NAME: *OCYCEROS GRISEUS*

Smaller but similar in structure and habits to the Indian Grey Hornbill, this bird is only found in the Western Ghats. It has an orange-yellowish bill without a casque. It has white streaks on its head, which appear to be bushy eyebrows. The tail is black, tipped white at the edge. The female's bill is more cream-yellow than orange.

BEST SIGHTED AT: Moist forests and woods along Western Ghats.

Clement M. Francis

ORIENTAL PIED HORNBILL (AROUND 58 CM)
SCIENTIFIC NAME: *ANTHRACOCEROS ALBIROSTRIS*

A huge cream-coloured casque edged with black sits pretty like a bayonet on the large yellow bill of this black hornbill. There is a white brush stroke right below its eyes. It has white under parts and its wings and long tail have a white border. The female's bill has a black tip. It makes different kind of shrill sounds.

BEST SIGHTED AT: Forests, fruiting trees, and near cultivation.

Debashis Deb

16

GREAT HORNBILL (AROUND 100 CM)
SCIENTIFIC NAME: *BUCEROS BICORNIS*

Joydip & Suchandra Kundu

This is a massive black bird with a flat yellow casque sitting atop its yellow bill. A yellow tint runs along its white neck as well as on the tail feathers. The black wings have a yellow and white bar and a white border, which become more prominent during flight. The white tail is punctured with a black band towards the end. Its loud calls can be heard from far away.

BEST SIGHTED AT: Fruiting trees and forests.

UPUPIFORMES

COMMON HOOPOE
(AROUND 31 CM)
SCIENTIFIC NAME: *UPUPA EPOPS*

Many think this is another woodpecker, which it is not. This is an orange-brown bird with black and white zebra markings on its wings. It has a royal fan-like crest tipped with black and a characteristic long pointed bill. It is commonly found digging ceaselessly and feeding on insects and worms in the ground.

BEST SIGHTED AT: Human settlements (especially villages) and cultivation.

Joydip & Suchandra Kundu

BIRD TRIVIA

MOST INTELLIGENT BIRDS:
African Grey Parrot, crows, 'bait-fishing' Green and Striated herons.

CORACIFORMES

Mike Vickers

INDIAN ROLLER

(AROUND 33 CM)
SCIENTIFIC NAME:
CORACIAS BENGHALENSIS

Also known as Blue Jay, this striking blue bird is a common sight around human habitation. It has a brown and greenish back, blue crown and belly, and buff and lilac streaks on throat. The neck and breast are light brown and the aqua-and-deep-blue wings and tail dazzle in flight. It perches itself on electric wires along the roadside.

BEST SIGHTED AT: Habitation, gardens, and cultivation.

COMMON KINGFISHER (AROUND 16 CM)
SCIENTIFIC NAME: *ALCEDO ATTHIS*

This kingfisher is also known as Little Blue. It has blue-green to turquoise upper parts with a white throat and side neck patch. It has orange ear coverts and under parts, and a long pointed blue-black bill. The head has dark blue markings and the tiny feet are bright crimson. Usually, it may be seen perched motionless near water.

BEST SIGHTED AT: Rivers and streams.

Satpal Gandhi

18

PIED KINGFISHER

(AROUND 31 CM)
SCIENTIFIC NAME: *CERYLE RUDIS*

This is a black and white kingfisher with a clear white supercilium and black bands across the breast. It sports a small bushy crest and has a powerful thick bill. Its characteristic hunting style is to hover in the air like a helicopter and then dive vertically into the water.

BEST SIGHTED AT: Rivers and lakes.

Satpal Gandhi

CRESTED KINGFISHER (AROUND 41 CM)
SCIENTIFIC NAME: *MEGACERLYLE LUGUBRIS*

A large black/grey and white kingfisher with a prominent crest, it is also known as Himalayan Kingfisher for its range and habitat. The head is marked from the rest of the body by a broad white band and there is a rufous patch near the breast. It has black ear coverts and no supercilium. It is seen flying low over streams.

BEST SIGHTED AT: Mountain rivers and streams.

N.C. Dhingra

BIRD TRIVIA

LONGEST WINGSPAN AMONG LAND-BIRDS: both Andean Condor and Marabou Stork at 3.2 m.

19

BLACK-CAPPED KINGFISHER (AROUND 30 CM)
SCIENTIFIC NAME: *HALCYON PILEATA*

This striking bird has a prominent black head with a big contrasting red bill. The head and the purple-blue body are divided by a thin white collar, giving the impression of it wearing a cap. It has a white throat, brownish under parts and red feet. It gives out a high-pitched resonating cackle *kikikikiki* and does not plunge into water.

BEST SIGHTED AT: Coastland areas and adjoining wetlands.

Joydip & Suchandra Kundu

WHITE-THROATED KINGFISHER
(AROUND 28 CM)
SCIENTIFIC NAME: *HALCYON SMYRNENSIS*

A common city bird, it was earlier known as White-breasted Kingfisher. With its brown head and under parts, red bill and turquoise blue upper body (including tail), it can be easily spotted. The throat and breast stripe are white. It survives on insects and small reptiles rather than a strict fish diet. The call is similar to a jarring laugh.

BEST SIGHTED AT: High-tension electric poles and wires; gardens and water bodies.

Joydip & Suchandra Kundu

STORK-BILLED KINGFISHER (AROUND 38 CM)
SCIENTIFIC NAME: *HALCYON CAPENSIS*

Debashis Deb

One of the bigger kingfishers inhabiting fresh water lakes, it has a brown head, buff under parts and collar with green-blue upper parts. A plump, multicoloured bird, it has an equally plump red bill with a black tip. It utters a shrieking sound *ke-ke-ke-ke-ke*, but whistles melodiously.

BEST SIGHTED AT: Running streams in forest and lakes in well wooded parts.

GREEN BEE-EATER (AROUND 17 CM)
SCIENTIFIC NAME: *MEROPS ORIENTALIS*

N.C. Dhingra

Sighting of this small green bird marks the arrival of spring and summer. With two prominent central tail feathers, it has bluish cheeks and throat marked from the rest of the body by a thin black line. The head is yellow-green in colour, there is a black eye-stripe, and the bill is thin and sharp.

BEST SIGHTED AT: Habitation, cultivation and villages.

BIRD TRIVIA | **SMALLEST BIRD:** Bee Hummingbird at 5.7 cm and 1.6 g.

CHESTNUT-HEADED BEE-EATER (AROUND 19 CM)
SCIENTIFIC NAME: *MEROPS LESCHENAULTI*

This bee-eater has a brilliant chestnut head, nape and mantle with a black eye-stripe. It has a yellow face and throat, bordered with rufous and a thin black line. The rump and belly are bluish on an otherwise green body and the tail is shallow forked.

BEST SIGHTED AT: Near water in deciduous forests.

Joydip & Suchandra Kundu

CUCULIFORMES

PIED CUCKOO (AROUND 33 CM)
SCIENTIFIC NAME: *CLAMATOR JACOBINUS*

This is a black and white bird with a prominent crest and white-tipped graduated tail; the outer wings have small white bars. It is a brood parasite and lays its egg mostly in the nests of babblers. Its call is a loud *pipew pipew*. The pied cuckoo is migratory and comes from East Africa, generally during monsoon months.

BEST SIGHTED AT: Well-wooded scrub forests, cultivation.

Debashis Deb

COMMON HAWK CUCKOO (AROUND 34 CM)
SCIENTIFIC NAME: *HIEROCOCCYX VARIUS*

Nikhil Devasar

Even before you can spot this bird you will be alerted by its well-known and persistent 'brain fever' call (a shrill and repetitive *pee pee ah*), for it is also known as Brainfever Bird. Its upper parts are ashy grey in colour and the belly is whitish, cross-barred with brown. The tail is broad and grey/black barred. It can be seen singly in wooded country and it is nest-parasitic.

BEST SIGHTED AT: Wooded areas, light forests, partial gardens, groves and mango trees near human habitation.

ASIAN KOEL (AROUND 43 CM)
SCIENTIFIC NAME:
EUDYNAMYS SCOLOPACEA

Satpal Gandhi

This is a crow-sized bird with a long tail. The male is shining black with a greenish yellow bill and red eyes. The female has a tinge of brown on black, with white spots all over. At the onset of spring one can hear its friendly neighbourhood call, *kuoo kuoo* at dawn with a consistently rising pitch. The female usually lays its egg in a crow's nest.

BEST SIGHTED AT: Groves or gardens, and large trees.

BIRD TRIVIA | **MOST ABUNDANT BIRD:** Red-billed Quelea at up to 1.5 billion.

GREATER COUCAL (AROUND 48 CM)
SCIENTIFIC NAME: *CENTROPUS SINENSIS*

This is a large bird with a purple-black head and body, shiny chestnut wings, and a long, dark green tail. Both sexes are similar, but the juvenile is duller and heavily barred. It is also known as Crow Pheasant or simply Coucal, and does not fly that much but walks heavily on the ground.

BEST SIGHTED AT: Wide range of habitats from jungles to cultivation.

Nikhil Devasar

PSITTACIFORMES

ALEXANDRINE PARAKEET (AROUND 53 CM)
SCIENTIFIC NAME: *PSITTACULA EUPATRIA*

This is a large green parakeet with red patches on its shoulder and a fat round red beak. Considerably bigger than the common Rose-ringed Parakeet, it also has a distinct, loud and harsh call. The male has a broad pinkish-red and blue band around its neck and a black stripe from the chin to the throat, which the female lacks. The long tail is tinged with pale blue above.

BEST SIGHTED AT: Flocks in parks and trees around habi-tation as well as in wooded areas.

Anand Arya

ROSE-RINGED PARAKEET

(AROUND 42 CM)
SCIENTIFIC NAME:
PSITTACULA KRAMERI

This is the '*tota*' we all know from school books, and is a light green parakeet. The male sports a pink ring around the neck and the same black chin stripe of the Alexandrine though it is smaller and lacks the red shoulder patches. It has a long blue-green tail and a red beak. The *tota* is generally found in flocks and is a noisy bird.

BEST SIGHTED AT: Fruiting trees, gardens, orchards, and wooded areas.

Clement M. Francis

PLUM-HEADED PARAKEET

(AROUND 36 CM)
SCIENTIFIC NAME:
PSITTACULA CYANOCEPHALA

The male has a prominent plum coloured head, while the female has a light grey head. The yellow of the bill tends towards orange in the male, which also has a black chin stripe, a violet collar and a dash of cherry on its shoulder. The tail of both sexes is a white-tipped purple.

BEST SIGHTED AT: Open woodland, gardens, orchards, and fruiting trees.

Joydip & Suchandra Kundu

BIRD TRIVIA
LONGEST LEGS: Ostrich, relative to body length; and Black-winged Stilt at 23 cm or sixty percent of its height.

Joydip & Suchandra Kundu

RED-BREASTED PARAKEET
(AROUND 38 CM)
SCIENTIFIC NAME: *PSITTACULA ALEXANDRI*

The distinctive male has a pinkish red breast and pinkish grey head, while the female's head is greenish and its upper mandible is black, instead of red. Both sexes have a black chin-to-throat stripe, yellowish inner coverts and blue-green tail. Mostly it is a quiet bird.

BEST SIGHTED AT: Open deciduous forests and bamboo groves.

STRIGIFORMES

Joydip & Suchandra Kundu

BARN OWL (AROUND 36 CM)
SCIENTIFIC NAME: *TYTO ALBA*

The barn owl is a nocturnal species residing in old and dilapidated structures as well as large colonial buildings. It is also known as Screech Owl for its sharp, screeching call. Just be alert for the screeching sound and follow it to its source at night. This owl is a medium-sized, yellowish olive-and-grey bird with a white facial disc and throat. The flanks are spotted with light brown and buff and the under parts are greyish.

BEST SIGHTED AT: Old buildings, bungalows, old forts and ruins. It can be a surprise visitor at your window ledge.

COLLARED SCOPS OWL

(AROUND 24 CM)
SCIENTIFIC NAME: *OTUS BAKKAMOENA*

Joydip & Suchandra Kundu

This is a distinct little owl with two little 'horns' as ear tufts. Surprisingly, it is the largest amongst all other known scops owls. The bird is grey-brown to white in colour with black streaks and a pale buff collar. It is quite evenly distributed in the subcontinent forests but because of its excellent natural camouflage, it is a challenge to spot it even in daylight.

BEST SIGHTED AT: Forests and well-wooded areas including orchards and large gardens. Generally other birds, especially crows, mob at it while it roosts in tree branches

EURASIAN EAGLE OWL

(AROUND 59 CM)
SCIENTIFIC NAME: *BUBO BUBO*

Clement M. Francis

This is a big, fierce-looking dark brown owl with prominent black streaks and long ear tufts. Its legs are covered with feathers and the eyes are bright orange. The facial disc is light brown with black markings; it has a white chin and throat. It is chiefly nocturnal and becomes active after sunset. The call is a haunting *huoohuoo*.

BEST SIGHTED AT: Rocky landscapes, cliffs and scrub habitat.

BIRD TRIVIA | **FASTEST-RUNNING BIRD:** Ostrich at 97.5 km/h (60 mph).

Mike Vickers

BROWN FISH OWL (AROUND 56 CM)
SCIENTIFIC NAME: *KETUPA ZEYLONENSIS*

The upper parts of this owl are blackish brown and streaked with buff or white. The throat is white, eyes yellow, and it has prominent ear-tufts. It has uniformly streaked sandy brown under parts. It is a nocturnal species, which can often be spotted roosting on branches during the day. It feeds mainly on fish and frogs.

BEST SIGHTED AT: Forests and wooded country—often near a water source.

SPOTTED OWLET (AROUND 21 CM)
SCIENTIFIC NAME: *ATHENE BRAHMA*

The stocky upper parts of this owl are grey-brown, heavily spotted with white, and the under parts are white, streaked with brown. The facial disc is pale and the eyes are yellow. There is a white neckband. This species is nocturnal but can sometimes be seen during the day.

BEST SIGHTED AT: Tree cavities and hollows in large trees like the *peepal*; open habitats including farmland and human habitation.

N.C. Dhingra

FAMILY: BATRACHOSTOMIDAE

SRI LANKA FROGMOUTH (AROUND 23 CM)
SCIENTIFIC NAME: *BATRACHOSTOMUS MONILIGER*

Clement M. Francis

The frogmouths are a group of tropical nocturnal birds related to the nightjars. This species is found only in the Western Ghats and in Sri Lanka. Large-headed, it has a large flattened hooked bill and a huge frog-like face. The male is grey and heavily spotted, while the female is rufous and lightly spotted. It rests upright on trees during the day, camouflaged by its cryptic plumage that can be mistaken for a dry branch. It is best located at night by its song, which is a loud, descending frog-like series of *klock-klock-klock-klock-klock*.

BEST SIGHTED AT: Dense broadleaved forests.

FAMILY: CAPRIMULGIDAE

INDIAN NIGHTJAR (AROUND 24 CM)
SCIENTIFIC NAME: *CAPRIMULGUS ASIATICUS*

Clement M. Francis

This is a small nocturnal resident breeder in India, Sri Lanka and all over Southeast Asia. During the day, Indian Nightjar lies silent on the ground, concealed in the soil by its plumage; it may be spotted in a strong beam of light. It has a dark grey-brown body streaked with black; the buff-spotted wings have a white patch each. It has a wide gape, long wings and soft downy plumage. Its call is a loud repetitive *chuk-chuk-chuk-chuk*.

BEST SIGHTED AT: Open forests, cultivation and scrub habitat.

BIRD TRIVIA | **SHORTEST LEGS:** Virtually non-existent in swifts.

Clement M. Francis

GREY NIGHTJAR
(AROUND 30 CM)
SCIENTIFIC NAME:
CAPRIMULGUS INDICUS

This is a dark grey-brown nocturnal bird with black streaks and spots; there is a small white throat patch. The male has four outer pairs of tail feathers with white spots, which are absent in the female. Its call is a repeated *chuckoo chuckoo chuckoo* with around five minutes' intervals throughout the night.

BEST SIGHTED AT: Forest clearings and scrub habitat.

COLUMBIFORMES

ROCK PIGEON (AROUND 33 CM)
SCIENTIFIC NAME: *COLUMBA LIVIA*

This is the pigeon on your window ledge. The white rump is its best identification, but the two long black bars on its grey wings are also distinctive. Overall grey, it has a shiny pink and green patch on the side neck. Rock Pigeons have been domesticated for several thousand years, giving rise to the domestic pigeon, which is able to return back home even if released at a location it has never visited before, up to a thousand kilometres away. Special homing pigeons have also been developed through selective breeding to carry messages.

BEST SIGHTED AT: Human habitation.

Ananda Banerjee

LAUGHING DOVE

(AROUND 27 CM)
SCIENTIFIC NAME: *STREPTOPELIA SENEGALENSIS*

Clement M. Francis

It is a long-tailed, slim pigeon, with a sandy brown upper body. The head and under parts are pinkish, shading to whitish on the lower abdomen. The rufous throat has distinctive black checks. In flight, the under-wings display a chestnut colour. The chuckling call is a low *oo-took-took-oo-roo*.

BEST SIGHTED AT: Human habitation, farmlands and cultivation.

RED COLLARED DOVE (AROUND 23 CM)
SCIENTIFIC NAME: *STREPTOPELIA TRANQUEBARICA*

Anand Arya

The back and wings of the male are maroon or purple-chestnut from which its name is derived. The head, neck, and rump of this short-tailed, plump bodied bird are blue-grey. There is a short black collar on the hind neck and the brown tail is fan-like. The female's back and wings are brown.

BEST SIGHTED AT: Open country, around human habitation.

BIRD TRIVIA | **LONGEST BILL RELATIVE TO BODY LENGTH:** Sword-billed Hummingbird at 10.5 cm.

Satpal Gandhi

SPOTTED DOVE

(AROUND 30 CM)
SCIENTIFIC NAME:
STREPTOPELIA CHINENSIS

It is a slim, long-tailed pigeon. The back, wings and tail are pale brown, heavily spotted with buff. The head and under parts are pinkish, shading to pale grey on the face and lower belly. There is a thick black neck patch finely spotted with white. The call is a low and gentle *coo-coo-croo*.

BEST SIGHTED AT: Dense broadleaved forests.

EURASIAN COLLARED DOVE (AROUND 32 CM)
SCIENTIFIC NAME: *STREPTOPELIA DECAOCTO*

It is a greyish buff coloured bird with a blue-grey lower back and wing patch. It has a black half-collar on its nape from which it gets its

name. Native to the Indian subcontinent and parts of Asia, it was introduced to other continents and now has a global presence.

BEST SIGHTED AT: Open countryside, cultivation and gardens.

Nikhil Devasar

YELLOW-FOOTED GREEN PIGEON (AROUND 33 CM)
SCIENTIFIC NAME: *TRERON PHOENICOPTERA*

A plump pigeon, it has a distinct yellow-green body with diagnostic yellow feet, and is commonly found in big flocks. The head is greyish with lilac patches on the shoulders and black outer wings. The mantle bar and tail are grey. Its voice is like a floating whistle, similar to other green pigeons.

BEST SIGHTED AT: Well-wooded areas, and banyan and *peepal* trees.

Joydip & Suchandra Kundu

GRUIFORMES

SARUS CRANE (AROUND 156 CM)
SCIENTIFIC NAME: *GRUS ANTIGONE*

Nikhil Devasar

This is the tallest and the largest bird of the Indian subcontinent and the only resident crane species found amongst all the fifteen endangered ones in the world. The elegant grey bird with a bright red face and neck sporting a white cap above is considered an auspicious sign indicating a good harvest and prosperous life. Its flight feathers are black. It is often found in pairs in a supposedly eternal bond and it makes a trumpeting sound in duets.

BEST SIGHTED AT: Cultivation and flooded fields.

BIRD TRIVIA — **DEEPEST DIVE FOR NON-FLYING BIRD:** Emperor Penguin at 540 m (1,772 ft).

33

Nikhil Devasar

DEMOISELLE CRANE (AROUND 95 CM)
SCIENTIFIC NAME: *GRUS VIRGO*

This crane arrives during the winter months in huge flocks. It is the smallest of all cranes with a black head and neck on a blue-tinged grey body and a plume of white feathers running from behind its red eye. The contrasting grey and black plumage looks beautiful in flight.

BEST SIGHTED AT: Cultivation and near large water bodies.

WHITE-BREASTED WATERHEN
(AROUND 32 CM)
SCIENTIFIC NAME: *AMAURORNIS PHOENICURUS*

This water bird has slatey grey upper parts and flanks. The face, neck and breast are pristine white, while the lower belly to under-tail is rufous brown. It has a short tail and yellowish green bill and legs with long toes for climbing over reeds and bamboo bushes.

BEST SIGHTED AT: Thick undergrowth by the side of water bodies.

Nikhil Devasar

PURPLE SWAMPHEN

(AROUND 48 CM)
SCIENTIFIC NAME: *PORPHYRIO PORPHYRIO*

This chicken-sized bird has a dazzling plumage of green, blue and purple. When it walks, it flicks its tail up and down, showing the white under-tail. The bill is red and extends to a shield on the forehead. The call is a loud, penetrating *kee-ow*. It is an excellent swimmer, but prefers to wander on the edges of the water.

BEST SIGHTED AT: Wetlands and water bodies.

Clement M. Francis

Nikhil Devasar

COMMON MOORHEN (AROUND 33 CM)
SCIENTIFIC NAME: *GALLINULA CHLOROPUS*

Secretive in nature, this species has an overall plumage of greyish black except the dark brown wings and white under-tail. It has a red shield-like bill with a yellow tip. The juvenile is brown all over and lacks the red shield. Its voice is a sharp, nasal *kurr-ik*.

BEST SIGHTED AT: Wetlands and water bodies.

BIRD TRIVIA   **LONGEST BILL:** Australian Pelican at 49 cm.

35

Anand Arya

COMMON COOT

(AROUND 37 CM)
SCIENTIFIC NAME: *FULICA ATRA*

The coot is a slatey grey bird with a black head and neck. It has a white *tilak* (frontal shield) on its forehead, a white beak and red eyes. It is seen in large groups in the winter months in water bodies, big or small. It has a variety of calls including a high-pitched *pyee*.

BEST SIGHTED AT: Wetlands, big and small water bodies.

CICONIFORMES

COMMON SNIPE (AROUND 25 CM)
SCIENTIFIC NAME: *GALLINAGO GALLINAGO*

The distinctive feature of this small, stocky bird is its long, pointed dark bill and dark-and-light stripes on its head. The body is mottled dark brown to black, while the throat patch and belly are white. Its back and upper wings show double-V stripes during flight. It rummages in soft mud, probing for insects and earthworms.

BEST SIGHTED AT: Wetlands and large water bodies along coasts.

Joydip & Suchandra Kundu

36

BLACK-TAILED GODWIT

(AROUND 40 CM)
SCIENTIFIC NAME: *LIMOSA LIMOSA*

Debashis Deb

This bird has a thin and pointed bill with a slight upward curve and pinkish orange at the base. The back is mottled grey on which the male develops rufous spots during breeding. The neck of the male is brick red, while that of the female is paler. The wings show a long white bar during flight. The face, neck and breast become sandy brown and the belly fades to white in both sexes during the non-breeding period.

BEST SIGHTED AT: Wetlands and large water bodies.

COMMON REDSHANK (AROUND 28 CM)
SCIENTIFIC NAME: *TRINGA TOTANUS*

Anand Arya

Redshank has bright orange legs and bill (with a black tip), and shows a white stripe on the back and white lower wings in flight. It is dull brown with black streaks and spots, becoming somewhat greyish in winter. A noisy bird, it will alert you with its loud piping call.

BEST SIGHTED AT: Wetlands and large water bodies.

BIRD TRIVIA | **FASTEST-RUNNING FLYING BIRD:** Greater Roadrunner at 42 km/h (26 mph).

WHIMBREL (AROUND 43 CM)
SCIENTIFIC NAME: *NUMENIUS PHAEOPUS*

It is mainly a dark greyish brown, with a white stripe on the back, and a long down-curved bill, which is crooked rather than smooth. It is mottled with white and buff. The under-wings are white with grey mottling at the edges. The familiar call is a hurried whistle.

BEST SIGHTED AT: Coastal areas.

Nikhil Devasar

EURASIAN CURLEW (AROUND 55 CM)
SCIENTIFIC NAME: *NUMENIUS ARQUATA*

The familiar call from which this bird gets its name is a loud *curloo-oo*. Overall it is greyish brown with small white marks, a white back-stripe, and a long, curved, pointed bill. It picks small crabs and earthworms off the surface if the opportunity arises.

BEST SIGHTED AT: Coastal areas.

Clement M. Francis

GREEN SANDPIPER (AROUND 23 CM)
SCIENTIFIC NAME: *TRINGA OCHROPUS*

Debashis Deb

A shy bird, this species does not like to socialise, although sometimes small numbers congregate in feeding areas. It has a dark green-brown back, greyish head and mottled breast, and a short bill. The back is spotted with white, more prominent during breeding. The white rump and wholly dark under-wing contrasting with white under parts are distinctive.

BEST SIGHTED AT: Wetlands, fresh water lakes.

WOOD SANDPIPER (AROUND 20 CM)
SCIENTIFIC NAME: *TRINGA GLAREOLA*

Joydip & Suchandra Kundu

It has a short fine bill, brown back mottled with white, a distinct white rump and spotted under parts. During winter the spotting fades. It maybe confused with Green Sandpiper except for the greyish white under-wing and several bars on tail instead of just two in Green. This bird is usually spotted amongst other waders during the winter migration.

BEST SIGHTED AT: Wetlands, fresh water lakes.

BIRD TRIVIA **LARGEST AND FLESHIEST TONGUE:** Flamingo.

Joydip & Suchandra Kundu

COMMON SANDPIPER (AROUND 20 CM)
SCIENTIFIC NAME: *ACTITIS HYPOLEUCOS*

You can spot the bird as its head bobs up and down while hunting for insects and other foodstuff. The species has greyish brown streaked upper parts, white under parts, short yellowish legs and a pale yellow bill with a dark tip. During flight the lower wings show a thin white bar. It utters a repetitive *wee wee wee*.

BEST SIGHTED AT: Wetlands, fresh water lakes.

LITTLE STINT (AROUND 14 CM)
SCIENTIFIC NAME: *CALIDRIS MINUTA*

This tiny wading bird is brownish-grey above and white underneath. In flight it shows grey and white sides to a pointed black tail and a thin white bar on the wings. It has a short and straight black bill. During breeding, it takes on rufous colouration all over with black streaking.

BEST SIGHTED AT: Sandy beaches, wetlands, mudflats, and estuaries.

Debashis Deb

Clement M. Francis

PHEASANT-TAILED JACANA (AROUND 31 CM)
SCIENTIFIC NAME: *HYDROPHASIANUS CHIRURGUS*

This regal bird has a long black arched tail and a greenish grey back. It has a white face to breast with a yellow hind neck bordered with a black stripe that runs from the crown. The non-breeding plumage comprises white under parts with a black breast band and eye-stripe, a white supercilium, and a short tail. It has huge feet and claws that enable it to walk on floating vegetation in shallow lakes.

BEST SIGHTED AT: Floating vegetation near water bodies.

BRONZE-WINGED JACANA (AROUND 30 CM)
SCIENTIFIC NAME: *METOPIDIUS INDICUS*

Ananda Banerjee

It is mainly a black bird with a striking bronze-green tinge to upper parts and wings and a chestnut-brown rump and tail. There is a striking white super-cilium, a yellow bill and a blue-grey forehead. The female is larger than the male. Young birds have brown upper parts.

BEST SIGHTED AT: Floating vegetation, water hyacinth.

BIRD
TRIVIA

SHORTEST BILL: Glossy
Swiftlet at just a few millimetres.

41

Debashis Deb

EURASIAN THICK-KNEE (AROUND 42 CM)
SCIENTIFIC NAME: *BURHINUS OEDICNEMUS*

Also known as Stone Curlew, this nocturnal bird is found in dry wooded and open areas. It is a brown streaked plover with 'thick-kneed' legs, largish yellow eyes and a thick round head. It shows black flight feathers with white patches in flight. Its call is a characteristic whistling *cur lee*.

BEST SIGHTED AT: Open woodland and cultivation.

PIED AVOCET (AROUND 43 CM)
SCIENTIFIC NAME: *RECURVIROSTRA AVOSETTA*

This is a stark white bird punctured with brushes of black on the back and wings and looks very striking in flight. With a black cap and a sharp upturned back bill, it has bluish grey legs.

BEST SIGHTED AT: Shallow brackish water or on mud flats.

Nikhil Devasar

BLACK-WINGED STILT
(AROUND 38 CM)
SCIENTIFIC NAME: *HIMANTOPUS HIMANTOPUS*

The red legs are the first thing you notice on this dainty bird. An overall white bird with black wings and a black patch on the crown, it has a straight black bill. It lets out a repeated high-pitched barking call.

BEST SIGHTED AT: Across water bodies.

Joydip & Suchandra Kundu

LITTLE RINGED PLOVER (AROUND 16 CM)
SCIENTIFIC NAME: *CHARADRIUS DUBIUS*

Nikhil Devasar

It has a small brown head, brown back, wings and breast-band, and a white belly. There is a white spot on the forehead and a broad white neckband. It shows a thin white bar on the wings and white tail sides during flight. In breeding it sports a black mask around the eyes and on the crown.

BEST SIGHTED AT: Mud banks near water bodies.

BIRD TRIVIA | **LARGEST EGG:** Ostrich measuring 17.8 cm by 14 cm (7 inches by 4.5 inches).

Joydip & Suchandra Kundu

YELLOW WATTLED LAPWING

(AROUND 27 CM)
SCIENTIFIC NAME:
VANELLUS MALARBARICUS

It is a pale brown bird with a black crown, long white supercilium and large yellow facial wattles. The under parts are white, as is the black-tipped tail. In flight, the upper wings have black flight feathers and brown coverts separated by a white bar. It has a strong *cheet cheet* sound.

BEST SIGHTED AT: Open woodland and cultivation.

RED WATTLED LAPWING (AROUND 34 CM)

SCIENTIFIC NAME: *VANELLUS INDICUS*

It is called the 'sentinel of the forest' because of its constant *tit-ee-tit-ee-tit.* It has a black head to breast with white cheeks and side neck stripe. The flanks, belly and tail are white. The wings and back are light brown with black flight feathers and a white wing bar. The bill, facial wattles and forehead are red.

BEST SIGHTED AT: Open woodland, cultivation, and near water.

Joydip & Suchandra Kundu

RIVER LAPWING

(AROUND 31 CM)
SCIENTIFIC NAME: *VANELLUS DUVAUCELII*

Satpal Gandhi

It has black legs, bill, head to nape and throat, with grey face and breast. The upper body is sandy-brown with faint blue-grey brushes. Its black flight feathers have a white wing bar and the white belly has a black patch in the centre which is distinctive.

BEST SIGHTED AT: Stony riverbeds, sandbanks, and *jheels*.

Nikhil Devasar

INDIAN COURSER (AROUND 23 CM)
SCIENTIFIC NAME: *CURSORIUS COROMANDELICUS*

This bird's population is declining at an alarming rate due to loss of habitat. It has a striking orange-brown crown bordered with black and white stripes extending from bill to nape. It has an orange neck and breast extending to a black belly. The wings are grey with black flight feathers seen during flight.

BEST SIGHTED AT: Open dry plains and cultivation.

BIRD TRIVIA | **FASTEST UNDERWATER SWIMMING BIRD:** Gentoo Penguin at 36 km/h (22.3 mph).

45

Clement M. Francis

SMALL PRANTICOLE
(AROUND 18 CM)
SCIENTIFIC NAME:
GLAREOLA LACTEA

This is a small sandy grey bird with black under-wing coverts and a distinct semicircular black tail patch seen during flight. Both the upper- and under-wings have a white and black bar. The throat has a buff tinge during breeding. It has a shrill rattling sound.

BEST SIGHTED AT: Sandbanks of lakes and water bodies.

BROWN-HEADED GULL (AROUND 42 CM)
SCIENTIFIC NAME: *LARUS BRUNNICEPHALUS*

This bird is highly active in winter, both when feeding and roosting in the evening. It is a bold and opportunist feeder, which will scavenge in towns or take invertebrates in ploughed fields. In summer it has a pale brown head to throat, but at all times a pale grey body with black wing edges, a white tail and red bill and legs. In winter, the brown hood turns into dark vertical streaks.

BEST SIGHTED AT: Wetlands and large water bodies.

Nikhil Devasar

BIRD TRIVIA

SMALLEST EGG: West Indian Vervain Hummingbird at 10 mm (0.39 inches) in length and 0.38 g in weight.

Nikhil Devasar

BLACK-HEADED GULL (AROUND 38 CM)
SCIENTIFIC NAME: *LARUS RIDIBUNDUS*

In flight, the white marks at the edge of the wing are a good spotting sign. In summer it has a chocolate-brown (almost black) head and at all times a pale grey body, black tips to the wing feathers, a white tail and red legs. The hood turns into dark vertical streaks in winter.

BEST SIGHTED AT: Wetlands and large water bodies.

RIVER TERN (AROUND 42 CM)
SCIENTIFIC NAME: *STERNA AURANTIA*

A forked tail with long flexible streamers, and long pointed wings are the distinctive marks of this medium-sized tern. It has grey upper parts, white lower flanks, and a greyish white cap streaked with black (which becomes fully black in the breeding season). It has a short, shrill, repetitive call.

BEST SIGHTED AT: Rivers, lakes, and tanks.

Clement M. Francis

47

OSPREY (AROUND 57 CM)
SCIENTIFIC NAME:
PANDION HALIAETUS

Osprey is known for it fondness for fish. This dark brown fishing eagle has grey under parts and long, narrow wings, which gives it a distinctive appearance. It has a white head and face with a black band running across from the eye to the nape.

BEST SIGHTED AT: Fresh water lakes.

Nikhil Devasar

BLACK-SHOULDERED KITE (AROUND 33 CM)
SCIENTIFIC NAME: *ELANUS CAERULEUS*

It has smouldering red eyes and black shoulder patches (inner wing coverts seen in flight) from which it gets its name; the rest of the body is pale grey with a white face and breast. Black-shouldered Kite hunts by scanning grasslands for small creatures. It hovers in mid-air with great agility.

BEST SIGHTED AT: Habitation, perched on electric poles.

Nikhil Devasar

Clement M. Francis

BLACK KITE (AROUND 60 CM)
SCIENTIFIC NAME: *MILVUS MIGRANS*

The red legs are the first thing you notice on this dainty bird. An overall white bird with black wings and a black patch on the crown, it has a straight black bill. It lets out a repeated high-pitched barking call.

BEST SIGHTED AT: Human habitation.

BRAHMINY KITE (AROUND 48 CM)
SCIENTIFIC NAME: *HALIASTUR INDUS*

Brahminy Kite is an attractive bird, similar in looks to American Bald Eagle, but with a chestnut plumage. It has a white head and breast that are faintly streaked and black wing tips. The juvenile is browner and heavily streaked, but can be distinguished from Black Kite by its paler appearance, shorter wings and rounded tail.

BEST SIGHTED AT: Inland and around coastal waters.

Clement M. Francis

49

Nikhil Devasar

WHITE-BELLIED SEA EAGLE
(AROUND 69 CM)
SCIENTIFIC NAME: *HALIAEETUS LEUCOGASTER*

This slim-headed eagle is an overall white bird with dark grey upper parts, grey under parts and black under-wing flight feathers. The white tail is short and wedge-shaped with a black base. It has a grey bill. When it glides, the wings make a broad 'V'.

BEST SIGHTED AT: Coastal areas.

EGYPTIAN VULTURE (AROUND 65 CM)
SCIENTIFIC NAME: *NEOPHRON PERCNOPTERUS*

Egyptian Vulture is also known as Pharaoh's Chicken because it looks like a dishevelled chicken. It has a naked orange-yellow face and bill and a white body with black flight feathers with a white trailing edge. The tail is wedged and easily distinguished in flight. It feeds on rubbish and carrion.

BEST SIGHTED AT: Habitation and open forests.

Joydip & Suchandra Kundu

WHITE-RUMPED VULTURE

(AROUND 80 CM)
SCIENTIFIC NAME: *GYPS BENGALENSIS*

Once abundant, it is now a critically endangered species. A typical vulture with a bald head, long, broad wings and short tail, it often moves in flocks. It has a white neck ruff and grey upper bill. The adult's whitish back, rump and under-wing coverts contrast with the otherwise dark plumage. The juvenile is largely dark. It stays near the carcass for a long time before flying away.

BEST SIGHTED AT: Habitation and open forests.

Clement M. Francis

Nikhil Devasar

LONG-BILLED VULTURE

(AROUND 87 CM)
SCIENTIFIC NAME: *GYPS INDICUS*

The long black neck and head is an easy way out to spot these birds when vultures congregate on animal carcasses. It has a slim pale bill and a variable light to pale brown body with a ruff of white feathers around the neck. The flight feathers and tail are dark grey to blackish.

BEST SIGHTED AT: Human habitation and open forests.

BIRD TRIVIA **LONGEST-LIVED WILD BIRD:** Royal Albatross at over fifty-eight years.

Mike Vickers

RED-HEADED VULTURE (AROUND 85 CM)
SCIENTIFIC NAME: *SACOGYPS CALVUS*

Among all the vulture species this one is the easiest to spot by its red head, face and neck against a black plumage; there is a thick white ruff. It also has pale red feet. In overhead flight, look out for the distinct white thigh patches. Unlike White-rumped Vulture, it is not found in groups but in pairs of twos or fours.

BEST SIGHTED AT: Countryside around human habitation and open forests.

HIMALAYAN GRIFFON (AROUND 120 CM)
SCIENTIFIC NAME: *GYPS HIMALAYENSIS*

A huge and heavily-built vulture, this is much taller than the other three mentioned; it is also the most aggressive feeder. Its plumage is pale buff to grey in colour with black flight feathers and tail. The feet are yellowish, and pale feathers come out in streaks around the neck and shoulders.

BEST SIGHTED AT: All across the Himalayan range and its foothills.

Debashis Deb

CRESTED SERPENT EAGLE (AROUND 66 CM)
SCIENTIFIC NAME: *SPILORNIS CHEELA*

Joydip & Suchandra Kundu

It has dark brown head and body with a scaly appearance and the crest remains folded like a hood. The yellow lores around the eyes are a distinct field mark. The tail and underside of the (rounded) flight feathers are banded with black and white. It is generally perched on leafy trees from where it springs on its prey. It has a series of sharp whistling calls during flight.

BEST SIGHTED AT: Forests and well-wooded country.

SHIKRA (AROUND 33 CM)
SCIENTIFIC NAME:
ACCIPITER BADIUS

Joydip & Suchandra Kundu

It is a small hawk with uniform pale grey head and upper parts and white under parts barred with orange-brown. The larger female has a brown wash to upper parts, and yellow eyes instead of red. The juvenile is brown above and white below, with brown spots. It has a loud *titu titu* call and also shrieks *iheeya iheeya*.

BEST SIGHTED AT: Human habitation including cities and villages, and in forests.

BIRD TRIVIA | **LONGEST TAIL FEATHERS:** Crested Argus (pheasant) at 173 cm.

53

Clement M. Francis

ORIENTAL HONEY-BUZZARD

(AROUND 59 CM)
SCIENTIFIC NAME: *PERNIS PTILORHYNCUS*

The plumage of this bird is variable from dark brown to pale but it has a distinct long neck and a slender pigeon-like head. It has a grey face, white throat stripe and a longish tail. The male's under parts may be rufous-streaked, plain brown, or pale-and-brown streaked; it has a small crest on the crown. The under-wing flight feathers have clear grey and black bars. The female is darker above but has faint streaks below.

BEST SIGHTED AT: Forests and cultivation, and often near cities.

STEPPE EAGLE (AROUND 78 CM)
SCIENTIFIC NAME: *AQUILA NIPALENSIS*

A common winter visitor to the subcontinent, this massive dark brown eagle has rufous-tinged protruding head and neck; its small grey patch on the back is seen during flight. The under-wing flight feathers and under-tail are faintly barred. It has a black bill with yellow ceres. The under-wings and upper-wings of the sandy juvenile carry distinct white bars as do the edges of its tail. Sometimes, it catches prey from behind bushes or even by snatching from other birds.

BEST SIGHTED AT: Open countryside and near water bodies.

Nikhil Devasar

CHANGEABLE HAWK EAGLE

(AROUND 66 CM)
SCIENTIFIC NAME: *SPIZAETUS CIRRHATUS*

Clement M. Francis

As the name suggests, this bird has a variable plumage pattern according to the lunar phase. But it generally has a brown head and back with streaked white under parts. A prominent crest stands out with a round tail. The pale morph has sandy under-wing coverts and a barred tail. The dark morph is wholly blackish brown with a banded under-tail. It has a shrieking call.

BEST SIGHTED AT: Forests and wooded areas.

COMMON KESTREL (AROUND 34 CM)
SCIENTIFIC NAME: *FALCO TINNUNCULUS*

Nikhil Devasar

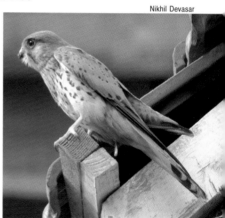

The male has a distinct grey head, a black-spotted rufous body and a plain grey tail with a terminal black band. The breast and belly are buff, lightly streaked with black—heavily streaked in the female, which is a black-spotted rufous all over with a barred tail. Lesser Kestrel female is smaller and lacks the faint moustache-like stripes.

BEST SIGHTED AT: Open countryside.

BIRD TRIVIA

LARGEST COLLECTION OF BIRD SKINS: British Museum of Natural History with 1.25 million.

LITTLE GREBE (AROUND 27 CM)
SCIENTIFIC NAME: *TACHYBAPTUS RUFICOLLIS*

Also popularly known as 'dabchick', it is the subcontinent's smallest water bird. Overall pale brown in colour with a white posterior, it has a dark brown cap and wings and its neck becomes chestnut during breeding. It is found in small groups swimming and diving close to the waterside.

BEST SIGHTED AT: Almost all water bodies from small ponds to large lakes and rivers.

DARTER (AROUND 90 CM)
SCIENTIFIC NAME: *ANHINGA MELANOGASTER*

It has a characteristic thin long pointed face and neck, which is the only visible part of the body while swimming. Its snaky movement earns it the name of 'snake bird'. It has an overall black body with fine streaking on the neck and a thin white stripe from the eye. It sits motionless on dead wood over water.

BEST SIGHTED AT: Wetlands, lakes and large water bodies.

Joydip & Suchandra Kundu

LITTLE CORMORANT (AROUND 51 CM)
SCIENTIFIC NAME: *PHALACROCORAX NIGER*

Nikhil Devasar

The head is somewhat rectangular in shape with a short bill which differentiates it from Indian Cormorant. It is mainly glossy black with white head plumes, silvery wing coverts and a longish tail. During winter it becomes dark grey with a whitish chin and the white spots on the neck disappear.

BEST SIGHTED AT: Wetlands, lakes and rivers.

GREAT CORMORANT

(AROUND 90 CM)
SCIENTIFIC NAME: *PHALACROCORAX CARBO*

N.C. Dhingra

It is a big black bird with a large wingspan. It has an angular head, a longish tail and distinct yellow spot at the base of the bill that comes in handy on the field. In breeding its head becomes white with a black crown and a black stripe runs from the ear coverts around the throat. During flight it shows a round white patch on the flanks.

BEST SIGHTED AT: Water bodies, lakes and rivers.

BIRD TRIVIA

LOWEST ALTITUDE FOR NESTING:
Little Green Bee-eater at 400 m (1,307 ft) below sea-level in the Dead Sea.

Joydip & Suchandra Kundu

INDIAN CORMORANT
(AROUND 63 CM)
SCIENTIFIC NAME: *PHALACROCORAX FUSCICOLLIS*

This is a slender black bird with a triangular head which makes it easy to identify from the glossier Little Cormorant. It has similar white forehead plumes and a whitish chin. The wing coverts are silvery with a longish tail. The non-breeding plumage is duller.

BEST SIGHTED AT: Water bodies, lakes and rivers.

LITTLE EGRET (AROUND 60 CM)
SCIENTIFIC NAME: *EGRETTA GARZETTA*

It has an all-white plumage with long black legs, yellow feet and a slim black bill. In the monsoon months when it breeds, the adult has two long nape plumes with red lores. In flight its legs extend well beyond the tail and the long neck is kept folded.

BEST SIGHTED AT: Water bodies, lakes and rivers.

Clement M. Francis

GREAT EGRET (AROUND 67 CM)
SCIENTIFIC NAME: *CASMERODIUS ALBUS*

Joydip & Suchandra Kundu

It is quite a large bird with an all-white plumage and can be distinguished from other white egrets by its yellow bill and black legs and feet. During breeding the bill becomes black with purple lores, and thighs develop reddish tinge. It stays motionless for hours to hunt prey in shallow waters.

BEST SIGHTED AT: Water bodies, lakes and rivers.

CATTLE EGRET (AROUND 50 CM)
SCIENTIFIC NAME: *BUBULCUS IBIS*

Nikhil Devasar

This common egret is often seen in rubbish dumps or taking a ride over livestock. It is a greyish looking otherwise white bird with a short thick yellow bill. It has rufous coloured head to neck and back and orangish bill and legs during breeding.

BEST SIGHTED AT: Cultivation and human habitation.

BIRD TRIVIA

LONGEST TAIL COVERTS: Indian and Green Peafowl at 160 cm.

INDIAN POND HERON (AROUND 44 CM)
SCIENTIFIC NAME: *ARDEOLA GRAYII*

Dipankar Ghosh

This stocky bird has a shortish neck, thick yellowish green bill and streaked buff-brown head and breast.The back is plain brown but in flight it looks white due to the wings' colour. In breeding the head to neck becomes plain buff with white nape plumes and a chestnut back. This bird found in abundance everywhere was first described by Colonel W.H. Sykes in 1832.

BEST SIGHTED AT: All kinds of water bodies and also around human habitation.

N.C. Dhingra

GREY HERON
(AROUND 94 CM)
SCIENTIFIC NAME: *ARDEA CINEREA*

The bird is largely grey above and off-white below with two black bars forming a 'V'. Adults have a white head and neck with a broad black band from behind the eye extending into a nape plume, which makes it easy to spot. It has black shoulder patches. It has a slow flight, with its long neck retracted into the body.

BEST SIGHTED AT: Water bodies, lakes and rivers.

Nikhil Devasar

PURPLE HERON (AROUND 84 CM)
SCIENTIFIC NAME: *ARDEA PURPUREA*

It is a large slender bird with a long snake-like neck. It is just a little smaller than Grey Heron, from which it can be easily distinguished by its darker reddish-brown plumage and black stripes along the crown and neck. It has a narrow yellow bill, which becomes brighter in breeding. Its neck is held in an 'S' stance in flight.

BEST SIGHTED AT: Water bodies, lakes and rivers.

LITTLE HERON (AROUND 44 CM)
SCIENTIFIC NAME: *BUTORIDES STRIATUS*

Nikhil Devasar

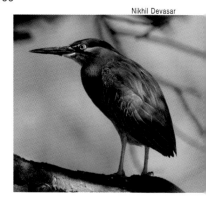

This is a small heron with blue-grey back and metallic dark green wings, whitish under parts, a black cap and cheek-stripe, and short yellow legs. It is also known as Little Green Heron. Juvenile birds are browner and heavily streaked. If flushed, it will fly over the water and hide amidst the foliage nearby.

BEST SIGHTED AT: Small water bodies.

BIRD TRIVIA **LONGEST TONGUE RELATIVE TO BODY SIZE:** Eurasian Wryneck at two-thirds of its body length.

Nikhil Devasar

BLACK-CROWNED NIGHT HERON (AROUND 61 CM)
SCIENTIFIC NAME: *NYCTICORAX NYCTICORAX*

It has a stocky grey body with short neck and legs and is mostly seen in the evening. It stands out with its black cap and back, and grey wings, rump and tail. The under parts are white to pale grey. The thick stout bill is black in colour with contrasting red eyes.

BEST SIGHTED AT: Marshes, streams and wetlands.

Nikhil Devasar

GREATER FLAMINGO
(AROUND 135 CM)
SCIENTIFIC NAME: *PHOENICOPTERUS RUBER*

It is always a great sight to see this beautiful whitish pink bird with its arched 'S' shaped neck. It has a large hooked pink bill with a black tip that is curved downwards. The wing coverts are deeper pink while the flight feathers are black. It is found in large feeding groups giving the horizon a pink hue.

BEST SIGHTED AT: Lakes, mudflats and saltpans.

BLACK-HEADED IBIS

(AROUND 75 CM)
SCIENTIFIC NAME: *THRESKIORNIS MELANOCEPHALUS*

It has a white body with distinct black bald head, neck, bill and legs. The curved bill is a prominent feature of the ibis family. There are white plumes on the neck and greyish on the back. The juvenile has a white neck. It forages for food in mixed parties.

BEST SIGHTED AT: Lakes, cultivation and wetlands.

Nikhil Devasar

EURASIAN SPOONBILL (AROUND 85 CM)
SCIENTIFIC NAME: *PLATALEA LEUCORODIA*

The bird can be easily spotted by its spoon-shaped long black bill ending with a yellow tip. The rest of the body is white along with a crest and black legs. In breeding plumage it has a yellow patch on its breast and a rufous throat patch. The juvenile has pink bill and legs.

BEST SIGHTED AT: Wetlands, rivers and lakes.

Joydip & Suchandra Kundu

BIRD TRIVIA

LONGEST-LIVED CAPTIVE BIRD: Sulphur-crested Cockatoo at over eighty years.

Nikhil Devasar

GREAT WHITE PELICAN

(AROUND 160 CM)
SCIENTIFIC NAME: *PELECANUS ONOCROTALUS*

This large bird with a massive wingspan has white (sometimes grey-white) plumage and a bare pink patch around the eye. The characteristic long bill is pink and blue with a hooked tip and a yellow pouch below. In flight, it looks elegant with the head held close to the body and the contrasting black flight feathers. It drives fish into shallower water and then scoops them into its pouch.

BEST SIGHTED AT: Lakes and water bodies where there are plenty of fish.

SPOT-BILLED PELICAN (AROUND 140 CM)
SCIENTIFIC NAME: *PELECANUS PHILIPPENSIS*

Clement M. Francis

A relatively smaller white bird compared to Great White, it has a grey head, neck and tail. The crest is blackish. During breeding the under-wing coverts become orangish, a yellow patch appears on the breast and the grey spots on the pink bill become prominent, earning it its name. The juvenile is brown.

BEST SIGHTED AT: Lakes and water bodies where there are plenty of fish.

BIRD TRIVIA

SHORTEST TAILS: Virtually non-existent in kiwis, emus, rheas, cassowaries.

PAINTED STORK

(AROUND 97 CM)
SCIENTIFIC NAME: *MYCTERIA LEUCOCEPHALA*

Its body is mainly white with black flight feathers, barred black-and-white wing coverts and pink tertials. The head is red or orange-red with a long down-curved yellow bill. Often seen soaring in the thermals with kites, it flies with its neck outstretched like a typical stork.

BEST SIGHTED AT: Wetlands and river basins.

Dipankar Ghosh

Nikhil Devasar

ASIAN OPENBILL

(AROUND 68 CM)
SCIENTIFIC NAME: *ANASTOMUS OSCITANS*

It is a white stork except for the black flight feathers. It has red legs and a dull yellow-grey bill. The mandibles do not meet except at the tip, and this gives rise to the name 'openbill'. It is much duller in winter. It also uses the thermals to soar.

BEST SIGHTED AT: Wetlands and river basins.

Joydip & Suchandra Kundu

WOOLLY-NECKED STORK

(AROUND 82 CM)
SCIENTIFIC NAME: *CICONIA EPISCOPUS*

It is a large black stork spotted easily by its long 'woolly' white neck and black capped head. The upper parts are a glossy dark green with a purple hue while the thighs and vent are whitish. It has a yellow-black bill and red eyes. The young birds are duller in colour.

BEST SIGHTED AT: Wetlands and marshy areas.

BLACK-NECKED STORK

(AROUND 140 CM)
SCIENTIFIC NAME: *EPHIPPIORHYNCHUS ASIATICUS*

It is a huge striking bird with a large wingspan. The head, neck, wing bar and tail are jet black, while the rest of the plumage is white, including flight feathers. Both sexes are identical except the female's yellow iris. The juvenile is mainly light brown with greyish legs.

BEST SIGHTED AT: Wetlands and marshy areas.

N.C. Dhingra

66

PASSERIFORMES

GOLDEN-FRONTED LEAFBIRD (AROUND 19 CM)
SCIENTIFIC NAME: *CHLOROPSIS AURIFRONS*

The leafbird is distinguished by its vibrant plumage, which is dense and fluffy. This bright leaf-green bird has an orange-yellow fore-head and blue shoulder patches. The throat is black bordered with yellow, while the chin is a deep blue-purple. It lacks the blue on its outer wings and tail as in Blue-winged Leafbird. It mimics other birds.

BEST SIGHTED AT: Forests and wooded areas; flowering trees.

Joydip & Suchandra Kundu

LONG-TAILED SHRIKE (AROUND 25 CM)
SCIENTIFIC NAME: *LANIUS SCHACH*

It has a grey head and mantle and a black mask extending from the forehead to the ear coverts. It has black wings and a very long black tail with a rufous base. The under parts are whitish with rufous flanks. The eastern race (*L. s. tricolour*) has a completely black head and mantle.

BEST SIGHTED AT: Cultivation and dry scrub areas.

Nikhil Devasar

BIRD TRIVIA **LOWEST NUMBER OF FEATHERS:** Ruby-throated Hummingbird at 940.

Nikhil Devasar

BAY-BACKED SHRIKE

(AROUND 17 CM)
SCIENTIFIC NAME: *LANIUS VITTATUS*

This is a small shrike with a maroon-brown back, pale rump and a long black tail with white sides. The crown and nape are grey with a black bandit mask through the eye, typical to shrikes. The wings are barred with a small white patch and the under parts are grey with buff sides.

BEST SIGHTED AT: Cultivation and dry scrub areas.

BLACK-HEADED JAY

(AROUND 33 CM)
SCIENTIFIC NAME: *GARRULUS LANCEOLATUS*

It has a black face and crest with a yellow bill. The throat is streaked black and white, giving the appearance of a beard. The body is pink-brown all over with blue outer wings and tail that have thin black bars. The wing coverts are grey and black with a white patch.

BEST SIGHTED AT: Temparate forests.

Satpal Gandhi

YELLOW-BILLED BLUE MAGPIE

(AROUND 64 CM)

SCIENTIFIC NAME: *UROCISSA FLAVIROSTRIS*

This is a stunning bird with an extremely long, flowing blue tail. It is usually found in small groups with its distinct black head to breast with a white nape-band and blue-grey upper parts. The under parts are white with a yellow wash. The bill is yellow and feet are orange.

BEST SIGHTED AT: Himalayan forests and forest clearings.

Debashis Deb

RUFOUS TREEPIE

(AROUND 48 CM)

SCIENTIFIC NAME: *DENDROCITTA VAGABUNDA*

An extremely agile scavenger, with a distinct black head, deep slate-grey coloured neck and breast, this bird's tail is grey with a thick black band on the tip. The back is deep rufous and under parts are buff with white wing coverts and grey and black outer wings. The bill and feet are black.

BEST SIGHTED AT: Scrub forests and cultivation.

Dipankar Ghosh

BIRD TRIVIA   **SLOWEST-FLYING BIRD:** American Woodcock at 8 km/h.

Nikhil Devasar

HOUSE CROW

(AROUND 40 CM)

SCIENTIFIC NAME: *CORVUS SPLENDENS*

This is one bird, which is found in all the nooks and crannies of the Indian subcontinent. Associated with folklore, it is overall a richly glossed black with lighter grey-brown neck and breast. The thickness of the bill and the depth of colour in plumage vary from region to region. A clever bird, it feeds on almost anything.

BEST SIGHTED AT: Human habitation.

LARGE-BILLED CROW (AROUND 54 CM)
SCIENTIFIC NAME: *CORVUS MACRORHYNCHOS*

This big crow species has a relatively long bill with a slightly curved, thick upper mandible, making it look bulky. Jet black in colour, it has a slatey grey tinge from the nape to the neck, shoulders and lower body. It has a loud and harsh *kaa-kaa-kaa* call.

BEST SIGHTED AT: Wooded areas and forests, especially in Himalayan regions.

Clement M. Francis

EURASIAN GOLDEN ORIOLE (AROUND 25 CM)
SCIENTIFIC NAME: *ORIOLUS ORIOLUS*

Joydip & Suchandra Kundu

The male is a bright golden yellow bird with black eye-streak, wings and central tail stripe. The wings have yellow patches. The female is duller and olive-coloured with streaks on the under parts. A common breeding summer visitor to northern India, this oriole can be seen singly or in pairs among leafy trees in wooded country.

BEST SIGHTED AT: Well-wooded country, forests.

BLACK-HOODED ORIOLE (AROUND 25 CM)
SCIENTIFIC NAME: *ORIOLUS XANTHORNUS*

Joydip & Suchandra Kundu

The male is striking with its black head over a golden yellow body. The wings and tail are a mix of black and golden yellow. The female has the black hood, but has greenish upper parts. A shy bird, its plumage makes it difficult to spot amidst the canopy of green leaves.

BEST SIGHTED AT: Open woodland and cultivation.

BIRD TRIVIA **FASTEST WINGBEAT:** Hummingbirds at 90/sec.

71

Satpal Gandhi

LONG-TAILED MINIVET

(AROUND 20 CM)
SCIENTIFIC NAME: *PERICROCOTUS ETHOLOGUS*

The male is a glossy black and scarlet arboreal bird with a characteristic inverted scarlet 'U' on the black wings. The female is yellow and grey in colour. Its distinctive *pi roo* whistling call and the red on the secondaries distinguishes it from the very similar Short-billed Minivet (*P. bevirostris*).

BEST SIGHTED AT: Open deciduous forests.

SCARLET MINIVET

(AROUND 21 CM)
SCIENTIFIC NAME: *PERICROCOTUS FLAMMEUS*

Found in small flocks, the sexes have distinct colouration. The male has glossy black upper parts and head, and scarlet under parts that are grey and yellow in the female, respec-tively. It is distinguished from the other two similar minivets by its larger size and the single circular wing patch.

BEST SIGHTED AT: Forests and other well-wooded habitats.

Debashis Deb

BLACK DRONGO

(AROUND 28 CM)
SCIENTIFIC NAME: *DICRURUS MACROCERCUS*

Joydip & Suchandra Kundu

It is mainly glossy blue-black with duller wings. The distinctive tail is long and deeply forked, and there is a white spot in front of the eye and bristles around the bill. It has short legs and sits ramrod straight while perched (mostly) on electric poles and wires.

BEST SIGHTED AT: Open woodland and forests and cultivation.

Joydip & Suchandra Kundu

ASIAN PARADISE-FLYCATCHER

(AROUND 20 CM)
SCIENTIFIC NAME: *TERPSIPHONE PARADISI*

The diagnostic long tail streamers make this small bird look double its actual size. It has a black crested head and throat, rufous upper parts and pale grey under parts. The female does not have the tail streamers and has a grey throat. The male occurs in another colour which is overall white with a black head. Both sexes have a bright blue eye-ring. In its flight it looks like a fluttering ribbon and is restless.

BEST SIGHTED AT: Forests and well wooded areas.

BIRD TRIVIA **SLOWEST WINGBEAT:** Vultures at 1/sec.

73

Joydip & Suchandra Kundu

COMMON IORA (AROUND 14 CM)
SCIENTIFIC NAME: *AEGITHINA TIPHIA*

The breeding male has black or greenish upper parts and bright yellow under parts, depending on the race; the flight feathers are black with a white wing bar, sometimes with yellow touches. The non-breeding male has uniformly greenish upper parts with a yellow forehead; the female is similar, but duller with greyish wings. It is told from Marshall's Iora by its lack of white tail sides.

BEST SIGHTED AT: Forests and well-wooded areas.

Satpal Gandhi

BLUE WHISTLING THRUSH
(AROUND 33 CM)
SCIENTIFIC NAME: *MYOPHONUS CAERULEUS*

This is a deep purplish blue bird with a yellow-orange bill and black base to lores. From a distance it looks almost black with whitish spots on the body and wings. It is often seen hopping about on the ground. Its song is similar to a low human whistle.

BEST SIGHTED AT: Near forest streams and in hill stations.

BLUE ROCK THRUSH

(AROUND 20 CM)
SCIENTIFIC NAME: *MONTICOLA SOLITARIUS*

It has an extremely variable plumage—from blue-grey to scaly blue to rufous under parts in the male, depending on the race or maturity. The female has brown scaly under parts and rough greyish upper parts. It has a shortish tail. It is found in abundance across the Indian subcontinent during winter.

BEST SIGHTED AT: Rocky habitat, mostly cliffs.

Clement M. Francis

MALABAR WHISTLING THRUSH (AROUND 20 CM)

SCIENTIFIC NAME: *MYOPHONUS HORSFIELDII*

It is dark indigo with a black head, neck and breast. There are bright blue patches on the shoulders and forehead. The juvenile has a black back and belly. The male has a melodious whistling call. It is a resident of the Western Ghats and the hills of peninsular India.

BEST SIGHTED AT: Near forest streams and gardens.

Clement M. Francis

Clement M. Francis

ORANGE-HEADED THRUSH

(AROUND 21 CM)
SCIENTIFIC NAME: *ZOOTHERA CITRINA*

The male of this small species has uniform grey upper parts, and orange head and under parts. The female and the young bird have browner upper parts. Both sexes have whitish wing patches. The race *Z. c. cyanotus* is a resident of the hills of southern India and the Western Ghats. It has a white throat and ear coverts with two black stripes below the eyes.

BEST SIGHTED AT: Forests and wooded areas.

RED-THROATED FLYCATCHER (AROUND 12 CM)
SCIENTIFIC NAME: *FICEDULA PARVA*

This winter visitor is mainly brown above and buff-white below, with the male having a grey head and orange throat. The bill is black, broad and pointed. The female and juvenile have a brown head. It often flicks its tail while calling or even cocks it above its head.

BEST SIGHTED AT: Forests and deciduous woodland.

Joydip & Suchandra Kundu

VERDITER FLYCATCHER

(AROUND 15 CM)
SCIENTIFIC NAME: *EUMYIAS THALASSINA*

It is turquoise blue in colour and has a clear dark patch between the eyes and lores, more prominent in the male. The juvenile has yellow-orange spots all over the body. Widespread in winters, it feeds above the canopy level and perches on electric wires or exposed branches.

BEST SIGHTED AT: Open forests and gardens.

Debashis Deb

GREY-HEADED CANARY FLYCATCHER (AROUND 13 CM)

SCIENTIFIC NAME: *CULICICAPA CEYLONENSIS*

It is a tiny, upright, long-tailed flycatcher. The adult has a grey head and breast, green upper parts, and bright yellow under parts. It has a short *pit pit pit* call and sings a high-pitched *chik wichee wichee*. It is a common winter visitor.

BEST SIGHTED AT: Forests.

Clement M. Francis

Nikhil Devasar

BLUETHROAT (AROUND 15 CM)
SCIENTIFIC NAME: *LUSCINIA SVECICA*

As its name suggests, this brown-grey male chat has a distinct bright blue throat band with a brownish orange patch beneath; in another race, the chin and throat are both blue with a round orange patch in the centre. The female has a streaked deep blue throat patch.

BEST SIGHTED AT: Cultivation; around reed beds along canals and water bodies.

Joydip & Suchandra Kundu

ORIENTAL MAGPIE ROBIN (AROUND 23 CM)
SCIENTIFIC NAME: *COPSYCHUS SAULARIS*

The male is a glossy blue-black bird with a white belly and a patch of white on the wing. It perches with its flickering upright tail. The female is similar but grey with a tinge of buff on the flanks. Its call is very melodious and it is often found singing in city gardens.

BEST SIGHTED AT: Human habitation, gardens and parks.

BIRD TRIVIA
COUNTRY WITH THE MOST NUMBER OF ENDANGERED BIRDS: Indonesia with 126 (Brazil second with 121).

Joydip & Suchandra Kundu

(Female)

(Male)

INDIAN ROBIN (AROUND 19 CM)
SCIENTIFIC NAME: *SAXICOLOIDES FULICATA*

The most striking part of this species is the chestnut-coloured vent under the upright black tail. The upper parts are dark brown, while the under parts are glossy dark blue to black in the male and grey in the female. The male carries a tiny white mark on the shoulder. In a racial variation the male has black head and upper parts.

BEST SIGHTED AT: Cultivation and scrub forests.

BLACK REDSTART (AROUND 15 CM)
SCIENTIFIC NAME: *PHOENICURUS OCHRUROS*

The male's plumage is quite striking: grey-black upper parts, sooty black breast and face, a rusty-orange red rump and tail, and orange belly. The female is a duller brown-grey all over with rust-red rump and tail. It is a common winter visitor.

BEST SIGHTED AT: Open country and cultivation.

Nikhil Devasar

N.C. Dhingra

WHITE-CAPPED WATER REDSTART (AROUND 19 CM)
SCIENTIFIC NAME: *CHAIMARRORNIS LEUCOCEPHALUS*

Overall it is a beautiful black and chestnut bird with a small white cap; the head, mantle, wings and breast are black and the remaining body is chestnut. This redstart is always active around fast-flowing mountain streams and is usually perched on rocks.

BEST SIGHTED AT: Mountain streams.

Nikhil Devasar

PLUMBEOUS WATER REDSTART (AROUND 12 CM)
SCIENTIFIC NAME: *RHYACORNIS FULIGINOSUS*

This is another small and stocky bird found along mountain streams. The male is overall grey blue in colour with a chestnut-coloured rump and tail, while the female is a dark grey with white rump and wing spots, and scaly brown under parts.

BEST SIGHTED AT: Mountain streams.

BIRD TRIVIA | **BIGGEST SOARING BIRD:** Albatrosses and condors.

COMMON STONECHAT

(AROUND 17 CM)
SCIENTIFIC NAME: *SAXICOLA TORQUATA*

A bird of open scrublands and grasslands, the breeding male has a black head and back and a white patch along the side neck. It has a white belly with rufous breast and flanks. The female and non-breeding male have a brown head

Joydip & Suchandra Kundu
(Female)

Anand Arya
(Male)

and back; while the female has a buff supercilium and rufous rump, the male has black ear coverts and white-rufous rump.

BEST SIGHTED AT: Open scrub habitat and cultivation.

WHITE TAILED STONECHAT (AROUND 13 CM)
SCIENTIFIC NAME: *SAXICOLA LEUCURA*

The male is very similar to its cousin, Common Stonechat except for its clear white belly and flanks and distinct white markings in its tail. The female too is similar, but is paler in contrast to the female Common Stonechat.

BEST SIGHTED AT: Tall grasses in reed beds near water.

Anand Arya

Joydip & Suchandra Kundu

PIED BUSHCHAT (AROUND 13 CM)
SCIENTIFIC NAME: *SAXICOLA CAPRATA*

The male is black except for a white rump, wing patch and lower belly. The female has dark brown upper parts and sandy to rufous under parts and rump; it lacks the wing patches. The juvenile is similar to the female.

BEST SIGHTED AT: Open habitats like scrubs, rough grasslands and cultivation.

CHESTNUT-TAILED STARLING (AROUND 20 CM)
SCIENTIFIC NAME: *STURNUS MALABARICUS*

It has dark grey upper parts, rufous breast and under parts and a chestnut tail. The mane-like head is a paler grey, with a white throat. Like most starlings, it is omnivorous. It flies in tight flocks and often changes directions rapidly in a synchronised manner.

BEST SIGHTED AT: Open forests and gardens.

Debashis Deb

Satpal Gandhi

ROSY STARLING (AROUND 21 CM)
SCIENTIFIC NAME: *STURNUS ROSEUS*

A common winter visitor to the subcontinent, the adult has a glossy black head, face and breast with a bushy crest and a pale pink body; the tail and wings are tinted with dark blue-green. It has a loud and shrill *ki ki ki* call.

BEST SIGHTED AT: Open fields and flowering trees.

ASIAN PIED STARLING

(AROUND 23 CM)
SCIENTIFIC NAME: *STURNUS CONTRA*

Nikhil Devasar

This is a typical black and white starling with prominent yellowish bill and legs. Its head is a distinct dark green with white lores and ear coverts and a red eye-patch. It is always found in small groups, commonly in cities. Its sound comprises various soft musical tunes.

BEST SIGHTED AT: Human habitation.

BIRD
TRIVIA

SMALLEST SOARING BIRD:
Swift.

83

Nikhil Devasar

COMMON MYNA

(AROUND 25 CM)
SCIENTIFIC NAME:
ACRIDOTHERES TRISTIS

This well-known noisy bird has brown body and wings, with large white wing patches. The head and throat are slatey grey; the bill, bare skin around the eyes and legs are bright yellow. Mynas come to roost in huge flocks and according to folklore, mate for life.

BEST SIGHTED AT: Human habitation and cultivation.

Anand Arya

BANK MYNA

(AROUND 23 CM)
SCIENTIFIC NAME:
ACRIDOTHERES GINGINIANUS

A little smaller than Common Myna, this bird is blue-grey with a black head, outer wings and tail, and reddish orange skin patch around the eye and bill. The inner wings are pale rufous and buff in colour.

BEST SIGHTED AT: Human habitation and cultivation.

BIRD TRIVIA **MOST AERIAL LAND-BIRD:**
Common Swift at three years without landing.

HILL MYNA

(AROUND 27 CM)
SCIENTIFIC NAME:
GRACULA RELIGIOSA

A popular cage bird renowned for its ability to imitate speech, it has a green-glossed black plumage, purple-tinged on the head and neck. There are large white wing patches which are seen in flight. There are yellow wattles on the nape and under the eye.

BEST SIGHTED AT: Forests.

Clement M. Francis

GREAT TIT (AROUND 14 CM)
SCIENTIFIC NAME: *PARUS MAJOR*

A broad black stripe (broader in the male) flows down its otherwise white front. The neck and head are black with white cheeks and ear coverts and a small nape patch. It has grey upper parts and a broad white wing bar. The young bird is duller without the black stripe on the side neck.

BEST SIGHTED AT: Open forests and gardens.

Joydip & Suchandra Kundu

Clement M. Francis

RED-WHISKERED BULBUL

(AROUND 20 CM)
SCIENTIFIC NAME:
PYCNONOTUS JOCOSUS

It has a tall pointed black crest, red and white cheek patch and thin black moustache. The tail is long and brown with white terminal feathers, and a red vent. It has brown upper parts and whitish under parts with a dark spur running onto the breast at shoulder level.

BEST SIGHTED AT: Human habitation, gardens and forests.

Joydip & Suchandra Kundu

WHITE-EARED BULBUL

(AROUND 20 CM)
SCIENTIFIC NAME:
PYCNONOTUS LEUCOTIS

This species is very similar in appearance to the Himalayan white-cheeked bulbul but is smaller and without a crest and with a larger patch on the ear coverts; it has a black head and throat. It has largely brown upper parts, buff under parts, and a golden yellow vent.

BEST SIGHTED AT: Forest edges.

HIMALAYAN BULBUL

(AROUND 20 CM)
SCIENTIFIC NAME: *PYCNONOTUS LEUCOGENYS*

This bird has a prominent brown pointed crest and a black crescent shaped mark below the white ear coverts. The head and upper parts are olive-brown with a black throat and grey under parts. It is found in small flocks around villages and human habitation in the lower Himalayas.

BEST SIGHTED AT: Himalayan foothills.

Debashis Deb

RED-VENTED BULBUL

(AROUND 20 CM)
SCIENTIFIC NAME: *PYCNONOTUS CAFER*

It has scaly brown upper parts with a small black crest on the crown, and a white rump. The nape may be black or scaled depending on the race. The breast is scaled or streaked brown and the rest of the under parts are white apart from the red vent.

BEST SIGHTED AT: Human habitation and gardens.

Joydip & Suchandra Kundu

BIRD TRIVIA
LONGEST TWO-WAY MIGRATION:
Arctic Tern at 40,200 km (25,000 miles).

PLAIN PRINIA (AROUND 13 CM)
SCIENTIFIC NAME: *PRINIA INORNATA*

Clement M. Francis

It has short rounded wings, a long tail, and a short black bill. In breeding plumage, the adult is a grey-brown above, with a short buff supercilium and rufous fringes on the closed wings. The under parts are whitish washed with buff. The winter plumage is wholly rufous-brown with orangish flanks.

BEST SIGHTED AT: Tall grass and reed beds.

Nikhil Devasar

ASHY PRINIA (AROUND 13 CM)
SCIENTIFIC NAME: *PRINIA SOCIALIS*

It has short rounded wings, a longish tail, and a short black bill. In breeding plumage, the adult is an ash grey from the head to mantle without the supercilium. In non-breeding plumage, its mantle also becomes brown like the wings and a short white supercilium emerges. The under parts are orangish buff.

BEST SIGHTED AT: Cultivation and forest edges.

ZITTING CISTICOLA

(AROUND 10 CM)
SCIENTIFIC NAME: *CISTICOLA JUNCIDIS*

This bird gets its name from the frequent flicking of its broad, white-tipped tail. It is buff above with black streaks and a rufous back, while the under parts are whitish. During breeding, it develops rufous colouration on mantle and the crown becomes plain brownish.

BEST SIGHTED AT: Reed beds and grasslands.

Clement M. Francis

ORIENTAL WHITE-EYE

(AROUND 10 CM)
SCIENTIFIC NAME: *ZOSTEROPS PALPEBROSUS*

This is a tiny yellow-green bird with a prominent white eye ring and its under parts are white except for a bright yellow throat and breast. It is found in flocks and is very active in the dense undergrowth, often hanging upside down from flowers.

BEST SIGHTED AT: Forests and gardens.

Joydip & Suchandra Kundu

BIRD TRIVIA **LONGEST MIGRATION (ALONG A COASTAL ROUTE):** Common Tern at 26,000 km (16,210 miles).

Clement M. Francis

BLYTH'S REED WARBLER

(AROUND 14 CM)
SCIENTIFIC NAME:
ACROCEPHALUS DUMETORUM

A common winter visitor to the sub-continent, the adult has a plain olive-brown back and pale under parts. The bill is slim and pointed. It makes a few clicking sounds with the tongue before whistling its song. This bird is named after British zoologist Edward Blyth.

BEST SIGHTED AT: Scrubs or clearings, often near water.

Anand Arya

CLAMOROUS REED WARBLER

(AROUND 19 CM)
SCIENTIFIC NAME:
ACROCEPHALUS STENTOREUS

A comparatively large thrush, the adult has plain grey-brown upper parts and whitish under parts with sandy flanks. The forehead is flattened with buff lores, and the bill is strong and pointed. It has a resonating call and a loud melodious song; the male often sings in the breeding season.

BEST SIGHTED AT: Reed beds.

COMMON TAILORBIRD (AROUND 13 CM)
SCIENTIFIC NAME: *ORTHOTOMUS SUTORIUS*

Anand Arya

This bird 'tailors' its nest by sewing the edges of a large leaf together with plant fibre or spider webs to make a cradle in which the actual grass nest is built. A bright bird, it has vivid green upper parts with a chestnut crown and whitish under parts. It has short rounded wings and a long, slightly curved bill. In a racial variation, the male has pale orangish under parts.

BEST SIGHTED AT: Forests and woodland.

COMMON CHIFFCHAF (AROUND 11 CM)
SCIENTIFIC NAME: *PHYLLOSCOPUS COLLYBITA*

A common winter visitor, it is greenish brown or grey above and pale olive or off-white below (depending on race). It likes to dip its tail frequently. This warbler gets its name from its call, which is a repetitive cheerful *chiff-chaff*.

BEST SIGHTED AT: Wooded country near water and cultivation.

Anand Arya

BIRD TRIVIA | **MOST AQUATIC BIRD:** Penguins with seventy-five percent of their lives spent in the sea.

Dipankar Ghosh

WHITE-CRESTED LAUGHINGTHRUSH

(AROUND 28 CM)
SCIENTIFIC NAME: *GARRULAX LEUCOLOPHUS*

Reddish brown with a bulky white crest, this laughing-thrush has a fluffy plumage and short wings. The head and breast are snow-white with a black mask over the eye and the mantle is rufous while the wings and tail are brown. It performs acrobatics between the loops of creepers and hops about. The call is a loud, harsh chattering or a laughing song.

BEST SIGHTED AT: Forests and undergrowth.

WHITE-THROATED LAUGHINGTHRUSH (AROUND 28 CM)
SCIENTIFIC NAME: *GARRULAX ALBOGULARIS*

This brown laughing-thrush has a distinct white throat, grey breast and a prominent black eye patch. The belly is orange-brown and the tail has thin white sides. It makes buzzing calls and other sudden shrill sounds.

BEST SIGHTED AT: Broadleaved forests of the Himalayan foothills.

Nikhil Devasar

Joydip & Suchandra Kundu

Nikhil Devasar

STREAKED LAUGHINGTHRUSH (AROUND 20 CM)
SCIENTIFIC NAME: *GARRULAX LINEATUS*

Its flock is a noisy bunch of brown-grey birds with fine streaking, often found in open habitats. One race is grey with rufous streaking and it is vice-versa for the other race. The characteristic laughing calls are often the best indication of presence. It is found in large groups.

BEST SIGHTED AT: Cultivation, scrubs and wayside undergrowth.

COMMON BABBLER (AROUND 23 CM)
SCIENTIFIC NAME: *TURDOIDES CAUDATUS*

Nikhil Devasar

An overall sandy brown bird sporting a long-tail, it has dark streaking on the upper parts and is plain white on the under parts. Small parties of the bird feed on the ground in scrublands, uttering low warbling sounds and whistles.

BEST SIGHTED AT: Cultivation, gardens, and near human habitation.

BIRD TRIVIA | **GREATEST NUMBER OF FEATHERS:** Whistling Swan at 25,216.

93

Clement M. Francis

YELLOW-EYED BABBLER

(AROUND 18 CM)
SCIENTIFIC NAME: *CHRYSOMMA SINENSE*

It is rufous-brown above with white chin, throat, and breast, and a long brown tail; the belly has a rufous wash. It has a distinct orange eye rim with a yellow iris. It sings from atop a grass stem in short repetitive trills.

BEST SIGHTED AT: Tall grass.

JUNGLE BABBLER (AROUND 25 CM)
SCIENTIFIC NAME: *TURDOIDES STRIATUS*

It lives in flocks and its continual chattering and chirping give it the tag of a very noisy bird. It has grey-brown on the under parts, with some mottling on the throat and breast and darker upper parts. The head is grey and bill is yellow. The race *T. s. somervillei* of Maharashtra has an orange-brown tail and dark primary flight feathers.

BEST SIGHTED AT: Forests, cultivation and around cities.

Dipankar Ghosh

ORIENTAL SKYLARK

(AROUND 16 CM)
SCIENTIFIC NAME: *ALAUDA GULGULA*

Its flight is remarkable as it rockets up into the sky and flutters with continual singing before descending to the ground. It is buff and brown in colour with black markings and a small crest.

BEST SIGHTED AT: Grasslands and cultivation.

Clement M. Francis

PURPLE-RUMPED SUNBIRD (AROUND 10 CM)
SCIENTIFIC NAME: *NECTARINIA ZEYLONICA*

This tiny bird has a medium-length thin bill curved at the tip and a brush-tipped tubular tongue, which helps it to feed on nectar. The adult male has a maroon face, neck, back, and breast-band. The throat and rump are bright purple and the crown and shoulder patch are bright green. The female and juvenile are a faint grey-green with a yellow breast and rufous-brown on wings.

BEST SIGHTED AT: Forests, gardens around human habitation.

Clement M. Francis

Joydip & Suchandra Kundu

PURPLE SUNBIRD (AROUND 10 CM)
SCIENTIFIC NAME: *NECTARINIA ASIATICA*

Its bill and tongue are similar to those of Purple-rumped. The adult male is a dazzling purplish blue. The eclipse male has olive-grey upper parts and a yellow breast with a blue central streak extending to the belly. The female has olive-grey upper parts and yellowish under parts.

BEST SIGHTED AT: Human habitation and gardens.

Joydip & Suchandra Kundu

CRIMSON SUNBIRD
(AROUND 11 CM)
SCIENTIFIC NAME:
AETHOPYGA SIPARAJA

The bright male has a dazzling crimson breast and maroon back; moreover, the fore-crown is green and malar stripe is purple. It has a bright yellow rump, an olive belly (grey in other two races), and bottle green tail (there is racial variation in shape and colour, as a smaller race has a purple tail). The female has an olive-green back and yellowish belly centre. It can drink nectar by hovering like a hummingbird.

BEST SIGHTED AT: Forests.

HOUSE SPARROW

(AROUND 15 CM)
SCIENTIFIC NAME: *PASSER DOMESTICUS*

Quite an extrovert, this noisy bird loves to dig into rubbish and wastes. The male has a grey crown, white cheeks and black lores and throat. Overall the male is rufous-brown, while female is buff—both with black streaks, whitish under parts and small white patches on wings.

BEST SIGHTED AT: Human habitation.

Joydip & Suchandra Kundu

CHESTNUT-SHOULDERED PETRONIA (AROUND 13 CM)

SCIENTIFIC NAME: *PETRONIA XANTHOCOLLIS*

It is also known as Yellow-throated Sparrow because of its bright yellow throat patch. It is brown-grey in colour with a dash of brown on the shoulders (more prominent in the male) next to the white wing bars. Its call is very similar to that of House Sparrow, but the song is more pleasant.

BEST SIGHTED AT: Forest clearings.

Clement M. Francis

BIRD TRIVIA | **LARGEST DOMESTICATED BIRD:** Ostrich.

WHITE WAGTAIL (AROUND 19 CM)
SCIENTIFIC NAME: *MOTACILLA ALBA*

Nikhil Devasar

There is much racial variation in this species, with very subtle differences. It is basically greyish black above and white below, with a white fore-crown and face, black cap and breast. During breeding, the head and breast are black (throat may or may not be), with the distinctive white face, and the back maybe grey or black with broad white wing bars. It has the characteristic long, constantly wagging tail of its genus.

BEST SIGHTED AT: Water bodies and river banks.

WHITE-BROWED WAGTAIL (AROUND 21 CM)
SCIENTIFIC NAME: *MOTACILLA MADERASPATENSIS*

This is a slender bird, with the characteristic long, wagging tail. It has black upper parts, head and breast, with a white supercilium and large white wing bar. The remaining under parts are white. This is the largest wagtail species and is often found perched on water tanks in residential buildings.

BEST SIGHTED AT: Water bodies, streams, and river banks.

Clement M. Francis

98

CITRINE WAGTAIL (AROUND 19 CM)
SCIENTIFIC NAME: *MOTACILLA CITREOLA*

The adult breeding male has a black or grey back (depending on race) with bright yellow head and under parts. In first-winter plumage, the male's yellow under parts may be diluted with white, and the head have a grey cast. The female is grey above with yellow face and under parts. The juvenile has brownish face and flanks.

BEST SIGHTED AT: Water bodies.

Nikhil Devasar

YELLOW WAGTAIL (AROUND 18 CM)
SCIENTIFIC NAME: *MOTACILLA FLAVA*

This wagtail spends much time walking or running on the ground. There is a lot of racial variation. Distinctive features of the male are yellow under parts, olive to green upper parts with dark ear coverts. The head may be grey, olive-green, or black with yellow or white supercilium (missing in only two races). The female is grey above and white below with an overall yellow wash.

BEST SIGHTED AT: Water bodies.

Nikhil Devasar

BIRD TRIVIA | **EARLIEST DOMESTICATED BIRD:** Junglefowls at 3200 BC.

Clement M. Francis

PADDYFIELD PIPIT

(AROUND 15 CM)
SCIENTIFIC NAME: *ANTHUS RUFULUS*

This bird is mainly streaked grey-brown above and pale below with breast streaking. It has long legs and tail, and a pointed dark bill. It feeds on the ground and when singing, the male flutters for a while before descending.

BEST SIGHTED AT: Open habitats, especially short grassland and cultivation.

BAYA WEAVER (AROUND 15 CM)
SCIENTIFIC NAME: *PLOCEUS PHILIPPINUS*

The pendulous straw nests are weaved by the male, partially to attract the female, who chooses it based on nest construction; once paired, the male completes the nest. The breeding male has a bright

yellow crown and breast and a heavily streaked grey-brown body; the ear coverts and throat are black (in a different race, the throat is whitish and breast is brownish). The non-breeding male has yellow only as supercilium. The female is overall grey-brown with dark streaks.

BEST SIGHTED AT: Tall grass and reed beds.

Nikhil Devasar

Nikhil Devasar

STREAKED WEAVER (AROUND 14 CM)
SCIENTIFIC NAME: *PLOCEUS MANYAR*

This is a dark brown heavily streaked bird (distinctive) with a tint of yellow on the wings. The breeding male has a bright yellow cap and a black face and throat; otherwise, only a yellow supercilium and black ear coverts.

BEST SIGHTED AT: Tall grass and reed beds.

Male

Female

RED AVADAVAT (AROUND 10 CM)
SCIENTIFIC NAME: *AMANDAVA AMANDAVA*

Popularly known as Red Munia, the tiny male is a brilliant scarlet bird with a brown wash and white spots on the flanks and (brown) wings. The female is dull brown above with pale under parts and white-spotted wings. Both sexes have a black tail with a red base.

BEST SIGHTED AT: Tall grass and reed beds.

BIRD TRIVIA **KEENEST SENSE OF SMELL:** Kiwis.

Nikhil Devasar

INDIAN SILVERBILL

(AROUND 11 CM)
SCIENTIFIC NAME: *LONCHURA MALABARICA*

This small bird has a long black tail. The adult has a squat silver-grey bill, sandy brown upper parts, white rump and under parts, and dark wings and tail. It often found in flocks in the nesting colonies of Baya Weavers.

BEST SIGHTED AT: Dry open country and cultivation, especially near water.

SCALY-BREASTED MUNIA

(AROUND 11 CM)
SCIENTIFIC NAME: *LONCHURA PUNCTULATA*

A small but active bird that feeds mainly on seeds, the adult has a stubby dark bill, brown upper parts and darker brown head. The under parts are white with black scaly markings. The juvenile is a uniform plain brown with lighter under parts.

BEST SIGHTED AT: Open woodland and cultivation.

N.C. Dhingra

BLACK-HEADED MUNIA

(AROUND 11 CM)
SCIENTIFIC NAME: *LONCHURA MALACCA*

Clement M. Francis

The adult has a stubby pale grey bill, black head and breast, and rufous-brown upper parts. The under parts may be white with a black lower belly or wholly rufous-brown, depending on race. The juvenile is sandy with rufous wings that distinguish it from the juvenile Scaly-breasted, besides the bill colour. A conical beak helps it in eating grass seeds, which this bird specialises in.

BEST SIGHTED AT: Reed beds and tall grass.

COMMON ROSEFINCH (AROUND 15 CM)
SCIENTIFIC NAME: *CARPODACUS ERYTHRINUS*

The male is small and stocky with red upper parts and breast, with a faintly streaked brown back and white belly. The wings and tail are dark brown. The female is overall grey-buff with brown streaks. In the race *C. e. roseatus*, the male has a red back with brown streaks and the red extends to the belly; the female is also more heavily streaked.

Anand Arya

BEST SIGHTED AT: Cultivation and forest clearings.

BIRD
TRIVIA
KEENEST SENSE OF HEARING:
Barn Owl.

TEN NOTABLE BIRDMEN TO REMEMBER

JOHN JAMES AUDUBON (1785–1851):

American ornithologist and bird-painter whose 435 life-size paintings published as *Birds of America* was the most notable work of that time. The name 'Audubon' till today remains synonymous with birds and bird conservation (the Audubon Society) throughout the globe.

COLONEL WILLIAM HENRY SYKES (1790–1872):

An army officer, politician and ornithologist, his experience in statistical research in the army helped him in documenting natural history. He published his catalogues on the birds and mammals of the Deccan in the *Proceedings of the Zoological Society* in 1832. This included fifty-six birds new to science, including the Indian Pond Heron. The Sykes's Lark (*Galerida deva*) of peninsular India is named after him and one race of Blue-headed Wagtail (*Motacilla flava beema*) was given the common name Sykes's Wagtail in *British Birds* in 1907.

JOHN GOULD (1804–1881):

An English ornithologist remembered for his extraordinary hand-painted volumes on birds. His paintings are still considered as the finest works of bird illustrations ever presented; amongst them the series on hummingbirds, toucans and 'birds of paradise' are considered priceless. His most famous publications are *A Century of Birds from the Himalaya Mountains* (1831-32), the five volumes, *Birds of Europe* (1832-37) and the *Monograph of the Ramphastidae* (Toucans 1834).

THOMAS CLAVERHILL JERDON (1811–1872):

Jerdon started collecting birds shortly after his arrival in India as an assistant surgeon in the British East India Company. He published *A Catalogue of the Birds of the Indian Peninsula* for the *Madras Journal of Literature and Science* (1839-40). This included 420 species, almost doubling the list produced earlier by Colonel W.H. Sykes. Jerdon's most important publication was *The Birds of India* (1862-64), which included over a thousand species. He also wrote *Illustrations of Indian Ornithology* (1844), *The Game Birds and Wildfowl of India* (1864) and *Mammals of India* (1874). Jerdon was also instrumental in the publication of the *Fauna of British India* series.

ALLAN OCTAVIAN HUME (1829–1912):

A.O. Hume is popularly remembered as one of the founding members of the Indian National Congress. Salim Ali regarded him as the father of Indian ornithology. Hume accumulated the largest collection of Asiatic birds in the world, housed in his private museum cum library in Shimla. Most of his work based on this collection was lost when the manuscripts were disposed off as waste paper by a servant. After this huge damage the Hume's collection as it went to the British museum consisted of 82,000 specimens of 258 species. His noted works include *Nests and Eggs of Indian Birds* (1883) and *Game Birds of India, Burma and Ceylon* (1879, co-authored by C.H.T. Marshall), his quarterly journal *Stray Feathers*—a journal of ornithology for India and dependencies in 1872. His discoveries are now known as Hume's Owl, Hume's Wheatear and Hume's Whitethroat.

HUGH WHISTLER (1889–1943):
An English ornithologist who served with the Indian police in British India. Whistler studied and collected birds and his researches into Indian ornithology led to the publication of the *Popular Handbook of Indian Birds* (1928).

SALIM ALI (1896–1987):
The 'Birdman of India', Salim Ali was among the first Indians to conduct systematic bird surveys in India and his books have contributed enormously to the development of professional and amateur ornithology in India. He helped save the Bharatpur Bird Sanctuary and the Silent Valley National Park. Amongst his published works, the most notable remains the ten-volume series, *Handbook of the Birds of India & Pakistan* with Sidney Dillon Ripley, his autobiography *Fall of a Sparrow* and *The Book of Indian Birds*.

JAMES BOND (1900–1989):
The original James Bond was an American ornithologist, whose name was adopted by Ian Fleming for his fictional spy 007. Mr Bond was born in Philadelphia and worked as an ornithologist at the Academy of Natural Sciences. He was an expert in Caribbean birds and wrote the definitive book on the subject: *Birds of the West Indies.*

SIDNEY DILLON RIPLEY (1913–2001):
He was an American ornithologist. A visit to India at age thirteen with his sister included a walking tour into Ladakh and western Tibet. This led to his lifelong interest in the bird life of India. With Salim Ali he contributed immensely to the ornithology of the subcontinent.

HUMAYUN ABDULALI (1914–2001):
A cousin of Salim Ali, he put together a collection of birds from Bombay which led to the publication of a six-part series on the *Birds of Bombay and Salsette* in the *Journal of the Bombay Natural History Society* (1936-1939) co-authored by Salim Ali. His first publication was in 1931 on 'Eleven Koel Eggs in a Crow's nest'. He published 348 notes in his lifetime and his greatest contribution was the cataloguing of specimens in the collection of the BNHS. A new species of Nicobar Scops Owl (*Otus alius*) has been named after him.

TWITCHING

'Twitching' is a British term used to mean 'the pursuit of a previously-located rare bird'. The British term is said to come from the frenzy that descends on some when they receive news of a rare bird. The term may have been derived from one of its first proponents, who used to arrive on his motorbike in freezing weather in the early 1960s, still 'twitching' from the cold. The end goal of twitching is often to accumulate species on one's list. Some birders compete with one another to accumulate the longest species lists. The act of the pursuit itself is referred to as a 'twitch' or a 'chase'.

GROUP-NAMES OF BIRDS

(by Terry Ross at http://www.bcpl.net/~tross/gnlist.html & at www.mobilebayaudubon.org)
Some of these names are still in use, although they may be half a millennium old, while others are totally outdated. So, these collective nouns are simply for adding to your bird-collection!

1.   A badelying of ducks
2.   A bazaar of murres
3.   A bevy of quail
4.   A bouquet of pheasants (when flushed)
5.   A brood of chicken
6.   A building of rooks
7.   A cast of hawks (or falcons)
8.   A charm of finches
9.   A chattering of choughs
10. A colony of penguins
11. A company of parrots
12. A company of wigeons
13. A congregation of plovers
14. A convocation of eagles
15. A covey of partridges (or grouse)
16. A descent of woodpeckers
17. A desert or deceit of lapwings
18. A dissimulation of birds

19. A dole of doves
20. A fall of woodcocks
21. A flight of swallows (or doves, or goshawks, or cormorants)
22. A gaggle of geese (wild or domesticated)
23. A herd of swans, cranes or curlews
24. A host of sparrows
25. A kettle of hawks (riding a thermal)
26. A murder of crows
27. A murmuration of starlings
28. A muster of peacocks
29. A muster of storks
30. A nye of pheasants
31. A paddling of ducks (on the water)
32. A parliament of owls
33. A party of jays
34. A peep of chickens
35. A piteousness of doves
36. A pitying of turtledoves
37. A plump of wildfowl
38. A raft of ducks
39. A rafter of turkeys
40. A siege of herons
41. A skein of geese (in flight)
42. A sord of mallards
43. A spring of teal
44. A tidings of magpies
45. A trip of dotterel
46. A watch of nightingales
47. A wedge of swans (or geese, flying in a 'V')
48. A wisp of snipe
49. A wisp or walk of snipe
50. An exaltation of larks
51. An ostentation of peacocks
52. An unkindness of ravens

BIRDING RESOURCES

http://www.fatbirder.com/
Fatbirder – linking birders
worldwide . . .

http://www.rspb.org/
The Royal Society for the
Protection of Birds

http://www.savingcranes.org/
International Crane Foundation

www.indiabirds.com
India Birds

www.birdlife.org
Birdlife International

www.delhibird.net
The Northern India Bird Network

www.kolkatabirds.com
Birds of Kolkata & Bengal Birds

www.birdskerala.com
Birds of Kerala

www.orientalbirdclub.org
Oriental Bird Club

www.wetlands.org
Wetlands International (South Asia)
A/25, 2nd Floor, Defence Colony
New Delhi – 110 024

www.bnhs.org
Bombay Natural History Society
Hornbill House, Shaheed Bhagat Singh
Marg
Mumbai – 400 023

Bird Conservation Organisations and Institutes in India

www.saconindia.org
Salim Ali Centre for Ornithology
and Natural History
Anaikatty
P.O. Coimbatore – 641 108

www.indianbirds.in
Indian Birds
New Ornis Foundation
P.O. Box #2, Banjara Hills
Hyderabad – 500 034

www.wii.gov.in
Wildlife Institute of India
P.O. Box #18, Chandrabani
Dehradun – 248 001

www.wwfindia.org
World Wide Fund for Nature (India)
172-B, Lodi Estate
New Delhi – 110 003

http://envfor.nic.in/zsi/
Zoological Survey of India (ZSI)
27, Jawarharlal Nehru Road
Kolkata – 700 016

http://birdpoints.com/
A collection of observations of the
feathered bipeds resident in and
visiting India

BIBLIOGRAPHY

Bikram Grewal, Bill Harvey, Otto Pfister, *A Photographic Guide to the Birds of India and the Indian Subcontinent*. Periplus Editons (Hong Kong) Ltd, 2002.

Bikram Grewal, *Birds of the Indian Subcontinent*. Hong Kong: Local Colour Limited; 2000, 1995, 1993.

Richard Grimmett, Carol Inskipp, Tim Inskipp, *Birds of the Indian Subcontinent*. New Delhi: Oxford University Press, 1998. First published in the UK: Christopher Helm (Publishers) Ltd.

Salim Ali, *The Book of Indian Birds*. Oxford: Bombay Natural History Society, Oxford University Press, 12th revised and enlarged centenary edition, 1996. First published 1941.

INDEX OF **SCIENTIFIC NAMES**

INDEX OF **ENGLISH NAMES**

115